Fraser Island
Atlas and Guide

A Hema Outdoor Guide

by Rob van Driesum

Your ultimate guide
to the ultimate experience!

Discover Fraser Island

This is another in a series of outdoor guides, published by Hema Maps Pty Ltd and originated by Rob van Driesum. The guides complement the maps that Hema produces, with a focus on outdoor activities.

The Author of this Book

Rob van Driesum is a travel guidebook writer and producer who has explored Australia by 4WD, motorcycle, car and on foot. He is a former guidebook publisher with Lonely Planet and now works as deputy editor on a number of recreational vehicle magazines. He also teaches Media Studies from time to time and presents courses on travel planning.

He has authored, coordinated, compiled and edited guidebooks to many destinations in Australia and overseas. Fraser Island is his favourite place in Australia, though the Kimberley comes a close second and he also has huge soft spots for Tasmania, Far North Queensland and the coast of South-West WA. Talk about covering your bases!

Credits & Thanks

The author wishes to thank the following people for their invaluable support and advice (they'll know why he's grateful): Colin Anderson, Linda Behrendorff, Kaye Bishop, Elizabeth Blomberg, Angelo Comino, Adrian Davie, Iris Flenady, Gerry Geltch, Mark Reed, Annette Sargent, John Sinclair, Angus Tye and Kurt Weidner.

Change is Certain

Prices, schedules and regulations mentioned in this book are always subject to change. In fact, things change rapidly on Fraser Island as government policies are updated, the infrastructure improves or deteriorates, new facilities and services open up, and old ones get better, or worse, or close down.

This book can only be a guide and should not be taken as gospel. Read the latest advice and guidelines in the *Fraser Island Information Pack* that comes with your Vehicle Service Permit. These are updated regularly, so read them again even if you've already done so in the past.

Please Tell Us

We welcome and appreciate all your comments and any information that helps us improve and update future editions of this book. Please write to Hema Maps Pty Ltd, PO Box 4365, Eight Mile Plains, Qld 4113, Australia.

Or email us at: manager@hemamaps.com.au

Published by

Hema Maps Pty Ltd
PO Box 4365
Eight Mile Plains, Qld 4113 Australia
ph (07) 3340 0000
fax (07) 3340 0099
manager@hemamaps.com.au
www.hemamaps.com
3rd edition - June 2009

ISBN 978-1-86500-513-3

Copyright
Text & Maps
© Hema Maps Pty Ltd 2009
Photographs © Photographers
as indicated, 2009

Printed by
SNP Leefung, P.R.C.

Photographs
Front cover:
Waddy Point at sunset,
Photo Rob Boegheim
Lake McKenzie,
Photo Frank Stoffels

Back cover:
Sunbaking at Lake McKenzie,
photo by Rob Boegheim.

Publisher: Rob Boegheim
Editor: Natalie Wilson
Author: Rob van Driesum
Cartographer: Paul van-Cüylenburg
Designer: Debbie Winfield,
Natasha Muratidis
Researcher: Helen Meikle

National Library of Australia
Cataloguing-in-Publication entry
Author: Driesum, Rob van
Title: Fraser island atlas & guide
[cartographic material] / Rob van Driesum
Edition: 3rd ed.
ISBN: 9781865005133 (pbk.)
Notes: Includes index.
Subjects: Fraser Island (Qld.)-Maps.
Fraser Island (Qld.)-Guidebooks.
Dewey Number: 919.432

Contents

Fraser Island, the traditional home of the Butchulla people, leans out from the southern coast of Queensland and sweeps north towards the Great Barrier Reef. It is the largest island off Australia's east coast and the largest sand island in the world.

This magical paradise with its crystal-clear lakes, spectacular coloured sands, immense sandblows, lush rainforests, giant trees and abundant wildlife is a miracle of nature – everything here grows on sand. In recognition of its outstanding natural values, it is inscribed on the World Heritage List, one of less than 400 areas worldwide.

This place of exceptional beauty is tailor-made for an activity-based visit. Few areas in Australia are more rewarding when it comes to bushwalking, fishing, boating, four-wheel-driving, whale-watching, bird-watching or photography, which are just a few of the many things you can do here. Whether you're camping, renting a holiday house or staying at one of the luxurious resorts, Fraser Island will delight.

This book provides background reading, advice and tips to help you make the most of your visit. What it cannot do, however, is physically put you there. All that takes is the urge to fulfil a dream. Why wait? ∎

The Maheno

FRANK STOFFELS

Seventy-Five Mile Beach

Boomerang Lakes

Lake Wabby

Indian Head

Champagne Pools

Eli Creek

Waddy Point

Lake McKenzie

Chapter One

Backgrounds

Highlights

There are so many things to see and do on Fraser Island that it's hard to narrow them down to a list of 'must sees' or 'must do's'. One person's highlight may be another person's time-waster.

Fortunately the choice is such that everyone will find things to enjoy. Few national parks in Australia receive so many return visitors, which is testimony to the island's magic.

A somewhat subjective listing of the Top 10 attractions might read as follows, though not necessarily in this order:

Fraser Island Great Walk. This six-to-eight day walk strings together many of the island's famous landmarks, from pristine lakes and dense rainforests, to massive sandblows and the grandeur of the eastern beach. Less ambitious hikers can limit themselves to short sections of this world-class trail.

Central Station. One of the most accessible areas for visiting the dense, central forests. Immerse yourself in the unique rainforest environment along Wanggoolba Creek, and take a short walk to Pile Valley to marvel at 60m giant trees growing in sand.

Fishing. Try along the eastern beach, at Waddy Point, or in the west-coast estuaries. Anyone who enjoys fishing will be in heaven here.

Lake McKenzie. Crystal-clear water and bright-white sand, a spectacular example of Fraser's unique lakes. If the tourist crowds get a bit overwhelming, there are many quieter lakes just as attractive.

Lake Wabby. Watch a sandblow in action as it gobbles up this concealed lake.

Eli Creek. The largest creek on the eastern beach, a wonderful spot for a swim – simply let yourself float downstream.

The Pinnacles & Cathedrals. Brightly coloured sand cliffs along the eastern beach, sculpted into bizarre shapes by the elements.

Indian Head. Spectacular views from this high, rocky headland. Watch whales, rays and sharks in the sea below.

Wathumba Creek. Magnificent estuary on the west coast. A prime camping spot with glorious sunsets.

Sandy Cape. True wilderness area, with huge, windswept dunes and a sense of isolation found nowhere else on the island. Hard to get to but worth the effort.

Orientation

Fraser Island lies just off the south Queensland coast between Gympie and Bundaberg. It's 122km long and 5-25km wide and covers about 166,000ha (or 400,000 acres in the old money).

The widest part of the island is Cathedral Beach to Moon Point, the narrowest is the Sandy Cape Isthmus just north of Orchid Beach. The highest point is Mt Bowarrady, at 244m. The forested central highlands (or rather, dune ridges) lie between 100m and 200m above sea level.

There are no towns as such. The built-up areas are better referred to as settlements or maybe even townships, especially Kingfisher Bay on the west coast, which may qualify as a town to some people because of its wide range of services. Other large settlements are Eurong, Happy Valley and Orchid Beach, all on the east coast, along with the smaller hamlet of Cathedral Beach and the busy campgrounds at Dundubara and Dilli Village. The busiest place in the interior of the island is Central Station, no more than a campground and EPA office.

There are about 800km of trafficable roads, all of them sand except for about 40km of gravel and dilapidated bitumen in the south of the island (Dillingham's Road between Dilli Village and Ungowa, and the inland road between Hook Point and Dilli Village). About 200km of beach is trafficable as well, most notably the impressive eastern beach.

FRANK STOFFELS

Lake McKenzie

History

The sand mass that formed Fraser Island has been around for at least 800,000 years, and its dunes have the longest and most complete age sequence of coastal dune systems in the world. For more about this aspect of the island's past, see Geography & Habitats later in this chapter.

First Inhabitants

The first humans probably arrived on the island more than 30,000 years ago when it was connected to the mainland, camping here in the winter months when sea mullet was plentiful. Some may have stayed all year round, but, the permanent inhabitants didn't number more than a few hundred by the time European explorers and escaped convicts first estimated these sorts of figures.

In the peak season there may have been a few thousand on the island, divided into three groups – the **Butchulla** (formerly also spelled as Badtjala and other variants) in the centre and across onto the mainland; the Ngulungbara in the north of the island (an offshoot of the Butchulla claiming to be a separate tribe); and the Dulingbara in the south (another subsidiary of the Butchulla). The island seems to have been a popular corroboree area until the Europeans took over.

The Butchulla name for the island is Thoorgine or **Kgari** (also spelled K'Gari), pronounced "gurry". According to Butchulla legend, Kgari was the beautiful spirit who helped Yendingie, messenger of the great god Beeral, create the land for people to live on. Kgari liked it so much that she wanted to stay. As a reward for her efforts, Beeral turned her into an idyllic island with trees, flowers and lakes, and put birds, animals and people on it to keep her company. And so this beautiful, sandy paradise with its abundance of freshwater was born.

Much of the oral history relating to pre-European times has been lost, though elders and artists, such as Fiona Foley and Binnjubl, keep alive what they can. The late Olga Miller, an elder of the Wondunna group (one of the five current Butchulla groups), did a great deal as well.

Apart from information handed down by people such as these, we only have sketchy reports by European explorers and a few archaeological records. Stone tools and fish traps have been found, as well as many midden heaps (shell mounds) along the east coast. The middens betray a love of eugaries (*Plebidonax deltoides*, also known as pippis or wongs, from the Butchulla "ah-wong") – the triangular, bivalve molluscs that visitors today still dig out of the tidal sand and boil into a soup or throw on the barbecue. The oldest middens date back about 5000 years, when the sea level had risen after the last ice age.

Before then, the inhabitants simply walked across to what is now the mainland. Later, they resorted to bark canoes. Trees with canoe-shaped scars are still in evidence, with some good examples near Dundonga Creek and inland from Happy Valley.

Devastation & Deportation

The arrival of European settlers in the region spelled doom for Kgari's people. Less than a century later, every single one of them had been killed or deported if they hadn't succumbed to new diseases or hunger.

Escaped convicts in the early 1800s occasionally lived with tribes in the region, but in 1842 Andrew Petrie led a survey team to the Hervey Bay area and shortly afterwards settlers began to arrive in what was to become the Maryborough district.

They cleared land and established sheep runs and farms, giving rise to conflicts with the original inhabitants. The dense vegetation on Fraser Island provided refuge for Aborigines on the run – for a little while at least. The government retaliated with ruthless police patrols from 1850 onwards, most notoriously during Christmas 1851 when Commandant Frederick Walker took a detachment of troopers – including a contingent of Native Police from NSW – across to the island for a large-scale massacre.

Faced with the horrors of European rifles, diseases, alcohol and poisoned waterholes, Aboriginal resistance soon collapsed. The government confined Aborigines to Fraser Island and gazetted it as a native reserve in 1860, only to revoke this status a couple of years later to help the timber industry.

There were about 2000 Aboriginal people on the island in 1850, but their lot at the hands of the Europeans was miserable and their numbers declined rapidly. Only 500 remained in 1870 when Methodist minister Edward Fuller set up a mission at North White Cliffs, known to the Aborigines as Balarrgan – about 2km south of today's Kingfisher Bay Resort. Two years later, however, the mission was closed to make way for a quarantine station to process the large influx of migrants heading for the goldfields at Gympie.

By 1880, the Aboriginal population numbered only 230. Most of them had been moved to the mainland when the Queensland government decided in 1897 to ship them back to a re-established mission at Balarrgan. They settled into the old quarantine station, but soon came

Butchulla memorial at the Kgari Camping Area

into conflict with Maryborough day-trippers who liked to moor their yachts in the area. The government bowed to public pressure, and several months later the Balarrgan mission was relocated lock, stock and barrel to a far less inviting site at Bogimbah Creek, further north.

Bogimbah then became a repository for mainland Aborigines from all over Queensland, forcibly rounded up by the government and sent here from as far north as Townsville. This policy ignored their different cultural identities, and the strict discipline enforced in the harsh environment at Bogimbah made matters worse.

Nothing improved when the government handed the mission over to the Anglican Church in 1900. Attempts to enforce even stricter discipline failed, and many residents died from disease and malnutrition. In 1904 the mission was abandoned and the area became a centre of logging activity.

Most of the survivors were deported to Yarrabah (near Cairns) or Cherbourg (near Kingaroy), though an estimated 20 or so managed to remain on the island. They were rounded up and deported in the following years – the last remaining Butchulla, 'Banjo' Henry Owens, was sent to Cherbourg in the 1930s.

Many Butchulla descendants now live either at Yarrabah or in the Hervey Bay area. At the Korrawinga (Scrub Hill) Community Farm at Ninkenbah, on the outskirts of Hervey Bay, they have now transformed 30ha of barren land into a productive organic farm and busy arts and education centre. They still retain strong links to Kgari which the government recognises, and the

growth of tourism may lead to their renewed presence on the island. The Kgari Camping Area south of Cathedral Beach could be a start.

Early Exploration

Some historians argue that Spanish, Portuguese or Dutch explorers visited this area in the 16th or 17th century but so far it's little more than speculation. We do know, however, that James Cook sailed past in May 1770 and, unaware that this was an island, named it the Great Sandy Peninsula. He also named Indian Head because he saw many campfires there (natives east and west of Europe were often referred to as Indians in those days). He took depth soundings off Sandy Cape, which he also named, along with Breaksea Spit. The Butchulla in turn watched his ship's progress and created a song about a big canoe that was still sung at corroborees in the 1850s.

In 1799 and 1802, Matthew Flinders visited the island in the *Norfolk* and *Investigator*, respectively. He thought that Cook's Great Sandy Peninsula was an island but he wasn't able to prove it. He sailed down its west coast as far as Big Woody Island before the shoals barred further progress.

On his second visit, he landed at Bool Creek, about 4km south-west of today's Sandy Cape Lighthouse – the first European to do so. While the botanist Robert Brown traipsed through the bush discovering new plant species, Flinders befriended the local Aborigines, remarking on their fine physique and healthy condition compared with the Aborigines at Port Jackson. But like Cook before him, he didn't think much of the area itself ("Nothing can be imagined more barren than this peninsula"), although the many campfires along the coast (by which he could navigate at night) led him to suspect there was no shortage of drinking water – a useful note for future mariners.

(Flinders visited a third time, in 1803, after the *Porpoise* was wrecked on the Barrier Reef and he and 12 of his crew camped at Indian Head on their way to Sydney in one of the lifeboats.)

Twenty years later, Captain William Edwardson in the *Snapper* was looking for a site for a new penal colony. Unlike Cook and Flinders, he stuck close to shore (his instructions included a river location) and sailed into Tin Can Bay and on to Hervey Bay, proving Flinders' theory that the Great Sandy Peninsula was an island. Soon after, John Oxley sailed up the Brisbane River and the new penal colony became Moreton Bay, which developed into Brisbane.

Eliza Fraser

How did Fraser Island get its current name? Therein lies a tale ...

In May 1836, the brig, *Stirling Castle*, was sailing from Sydney to Singapore under the command of Captain James Fraser when it struck a reef several hundred kilometres north of the Great Sandy Island (as it was known by then). Fraser and the other crew and passengers, including his pregnant wife Eliza, took to two lifeboats and tried to get back to Moreton Bay.

Along the way, Eliza gave birth prematurely (the baby died) and the two boats got separated. Eventually the Frasers' boat landed near Waddy Point.

What happened next is unclear, as Eliza's version of events kept changing in her later narratives. It appears that the stronger survivors began walking south, leaving Mr and Mrs Fraser and the weaker members of the party near Hook Point, where they were captured or maybe rescued by the local Aborigines.

The group who headed south eventually met some Europeans on Bribie Island and they returned to Moreton Bay to organise a rescue. Meanwhile, those who had stayed behind were stripped of their possessions by the Aborigines and put to work. Or maybe the Aborigines tried to nurture them back to health, no-one really knows. The tough conditions took their toll and most of Eliza's emaciated party died, including her sickly husband (who was speared in her story).

After six weeks a search team from Moreton Bay arrived in the area and found two of the survivors at an Aboriginal camp at Noosa Heads. John Graham, a convict who had once lived with Aborigines here, set off in search of other survivors and found one of them at Hook Point.

Graham then tracked Eliza down at a corroboree near Lake Cootharaba in Cooloola. He convinced his former adoptive tribe that she was the ghost of his dead wife, and they escorted her back to the rescue party.

It was the stuff of legend and Eliza didn't let it go to waste. On her return to Sydney she fed off public sympathy with her lurid accounts of insufferable hardship at the hands of barbaric natives, and raised a considerable amount of money. She married another captain and returned to England, where she published a best-selling book and earned more money embellishing her story.

Eliza Fraser appears to have been a thoroughly unpleasant woman, but her stories resonated with public perceptions at the time and the Great Sandy Island soon carried her name.

JOHN OXLEY LIBRARY

Eliza Fraser, whose stories of her stay on the island were responsible for its current name

Unfortunately, her version(s) of the episode did little to help the public's understanding of the Butchulla and may well have contributed to their later mistreatment.

White Settlement & Logging

Andrew Petrie's 1842 survey expedition north of the Maroochy River in an overloaded boat explored Hervey Bay and discovered the mouth of what became known as the Mary River. Along the way the explorers found two escaped convicts 'gone native', including David Bracefell who claimed he had saved Eliza Fraser from certain death. Petrie also searched for James Fraser's grave on the island, without success, but in the process he noted magnificent stands of kauri and other timber and reported about them in glowing terms.

Within the year, settlers began arriving at Mary River and founded a settlement at Maryborough. However, the area was remote and Fraser Island even more so. It took another 20 years before a small team headed by an American, John "Yankee Jack" Piggott, began felling kauri in the south of the island, where some of the geographical features still bear his name. He was a ruthless pioneer who forced the local Aborigines into virtual slavery and by some accounts also forced himself on their women, and they speared him to death.

Other timber-getters followed in search of kauri, white beech and hoop pine. The discovery of gold at Gympie in 1867 increased the demand for timber, and bullock teams got busy hauling logs from the interior. Bullocks remained the main mode of transport until 1905, when a couple of Maryborough mills built a steam tramway to haul blackbutt and tallow-wood from the Poyungan and Bogimbah forests.

In 1908, most of Fraser Island became a forestry reserve. A few years later, Andrew Petrie's grandson, Walter, established a Department of Forests camp at Bogimbah and began a reafforestation programme. By now the Poyungan and Bogimbah areas were depleted, and the tramway was relocated to the mouth of Wanggoolba Creek in 1915 to allow access to the western tallowwood stands. The forestry camp followed a year later.

A NSW timber company, H McKenzie & Co., built a wharf at Balarrgan in 1919, along with a sawmill and a tramway to its logging areas inland. It was a huge operation, with rights to 10,000 acres (4000ha) over 10 years.

Meanwhile, the forestry camp at Wanggoolba Creek suffered from sand flies and poor soil, so in 1920 it was moved upstream to a far more agreeable location at what became Central Station. Five years later, the McKenzie enterprise folded due to financial difficulties and the Department of Forests took over its tramway and wharf, which it operated till 1937. The sawmill closed for good and milling was once again done on the mainland.

Until the mid-1920s, Fraser Island's unique satinay trees escaped the chop because the timber tended to warp when cut. But their high turpentine content was shown to make them resistant to marine borers, which, along with their enormous height (up to 50 metres), made them ideal for refurbishing the Suez Canal. They were soon used worldwide to line docks and as pilings for jetties.

The Bogimbah tramway terminus, 1911

JOHN OXLEY LIBRARY

ROB BOEGHEIM

Logging continued over the following decades, and by the late 1940s about 70% of the island's commercial reserves were gone. Meanwhile, the Department of Forests kept up its reafforestation programme, and in the early 1960s it set a logging limit of 24,000 cubic metres a year to match the regrowth rate.

Logging on the island remained hard work, however, and increased competition from plantations on the mainland made it even less profitable. By the end of the 1970s only one contractor still operated here. This coincided with the first proposals to put the island on the World Heritage Register, and the conservationist campaign gathered momentum over the next decade despite government resistance to the idea.

The anti-green Bjelke-Petersen government lost office in 1989 after a generation at the helm. A commission of inquiry looked into the future use of Fraser Island, which was officially nominated for World Heritage listing in 1991. After this, almost 130 years of logging finally came to an end.

Commandos could practise ship-boarding techniques on the Maheno shipwreck.

FRANK STOFFELS

Z Force Commandos

During WWII, Fraser Island became a secret training ground for elite commando troops known as the Z Force or Z Special Unit. The island's seclusion and varied terrain lent itself to both jungle and amphibious training away from prying eyes. There was even a shipwreck on the eastern beach, the *Maheno*, where the commandos could practise ship-boarding techniques and the use of limpet mines.

The Z Force was formed in 1942 to undertake missions behind enemy lines in the south-west Pacific, and over 900 men underwent training at their base at North White Cliffs. Most came from the Australian Army but some were British, Malay, Filipino, Dutch, New Zealander, Timorese, Singaporean, Chinese and free French.

Training was intense. The day began with an 8km run in full gear to Lake McKenzie and back, including a fully clothed swim across the lake. The men were taught jungle survival skills, unarmed combat and methods of silent killing. They became experts in plastic explosives, timing devices and booby traps.

Paddling and navigating a two-man canoe (folboat) over long distances was also part of the training. The men were taught to handle a yacht and to identify enemy ships and aircraft. Malayan pearl divers from Broome taught them colloquial Malay.

They undertook more than 260 operations behind enemy lines in Borneo, New Guinea, the Pacific Islands, Malaya and Singapore, some of which are still on the secret list.

Their most famous mission was code-named *Jaywick*, a raid on Singapore Harbour in 1943, when 11 Australian and six British men sailed from Western Australia in a small Japanese fish carrier, the *Krait*. Twenty miles offshore from Singapore, they launched three folboat teams who paddled into the harbour at night and blew up 40,000 tons of shipping with limpet mines. Then the whole group sailed back home intact. It was the longest and one of the most extraordinary sea raids in the history of war.

Not all raids were as spectacularly successful, and half of the 400 commandos who went behind enemy lines were killed in action.

Remnants of the camp are still visible at North White Cliffs – the flooring of the camp headquarters, the concrete contour map of Singapore embedded in the ground, and the old boiler on the beach which was used for limpet-mine training. A map of the site and other memorabilia are on display next to reception at Kingfisher Bay Resort.

Sand-Mining

The sand reserves in the Great Sandy region contain valuable minerals such as rutile and ilmenite (sources of titanium), zircon (many uses, including coatings in nuclear and chemical plants) and silica (glass and other products). Mining began in southern Cooloola in the early 1960s and extended to Inskip Point later in the decade, giving rise to the township of Rainbow Beach.

Several mining companies also held leases on Fraser Island and began to turn their attention there when the Cooloola reserves ran low. One of these, Murphyores, formed a partnership with the American giant Dillingham and, in 1971, applied for new leases in the south-west and north-east of the island. So did Queensland Titanium Mines (QTM), which had been operating at Rainbow Beach.

Thus began a bitter dispute between mining interests and an increasingly vocal group of conservationists, who formed the Fraser Island Defenders Organization (FIDO) to coordinate their campaign. The leases were granted and later that year, QTM began mining an area about 15km north of Hook Point and laid a bitumen road from the ferry landing.

Dillingham-Murphyores took a bit longer to get going, but in 1975 began mining in the south of the island as well. It established Dilli Village and built the gravel Dillingham's Road diagonally across the island to Buff Creek, just south of Ungowa.

Meanwhile, QTM had applied for new leases in the Bogimbah area. When the leases were recommended, FIDO appealed to the Queensland Supreme Court (unsuccessfully) and then the High Court, which upheld the appeal and in effect prevented further expansion of mining on the island.

FIDO's relentless campaign, appropriately symbolised by its bulldog logo, was now attracting interest domestically and overseas. In October 1976, the Fraser Island Environmental Inquiry – which was set up as a result of the federal government's new Environmental Protection Act – recommended that export licences should not be granted for any sand mined above Fraser Island's high-water mark. The government adopted the recommendation, which made sand-mining unfeasible and it ceased the following month.

The government also adopted the Inquiry's further recommendation that Fraser Island become the first area to be listed on the Register of the National Estate, paving the way for its eventual Word Heritage listing in 1992.

Tourists & Residents

By the late 1970s sand-mining had stopped and logging was on the way out but the island faced a new environmental threat – increased tourism and residential development. Some analysts have attributed this to the media exposure generated by the sand-mining and logging controversies, along with the island's World Heritage listing. Although these certainly contributed to public awareness, it is more likely that the major factors were increased wealth, the proliferation of 4WDs and, in recent years, the inexorable growth of adventure tourism not just among backpackers.

In the early days, tourism was limited by the difficult terrain and lack of facilities. Most visitors arrived in yachts and didn't venture much further than the western beach, or else they came to visit friends and relatives engaged in the timber industry. A small tourist village at Happy Valley in the 1930s lasted only a few years due to the Depression.

In the 1950s, Sid Melksham began operating a launch to the island and took visitors across to the eastern beach in his Model A Ford. He later acquired a lease at Eurong and in the 1970s and '80s developed it into the flourishing Eurong Beach Resort, which he eventually sold to the Kingfisher group.

Sir Reginald Barnewall set up a resort at Orchid Beach in the late 1960s, and even though he soon had to sell it, he opened up the northern part of the island to tourism (in 1993 the government bought and demolished the resort in order to help turn the north into a wilderness zone). By now, ferry services were operating to the west and south of the island and visitors began to arrive in increasing numbers – about 5000 a year in 1970. Holiday shacks proliferated as the government released crown land for subdivision at Eurong, Happy Valley and Orchid Beach.

By the late 1980s, visitor numbers had increased to 200,000 a year and there were several hundred permanent residents. The 65-hectare Kingfisher Bay Resort, three years in the making, opened in 1992 to wide acclaim from national and international ecotourism organisations.

Meanwhile, the government imposed visitor fees to help pay for camping facilities, road maintenance and other projects to reduce environmental damage. Unfortunately, this has not been enough to compensate for the rapid increase in visitor numbers in recent years.

The island now endures 400,000 visitors a year, split about 50/50 between independent travellers and organised tours. Unless they do their bit to help protect this precious environment, it may only be a matter of time before there's a cap on the number of entry permits issued to the public.

The inflow of permanent residents, currently about 300 depending on how you define 'permanent' (the Australian Bureau of Statistics says 1400 people were 'present' on the island during the last census), has been restricted by the fact that only 0.5% of the island is in private hands and the government is not releasing any more land. Real-estate values are relatively high.

Geography & Habitats

Some say that Fraser Island is to the world's sand masses what the Great Barrier Reef is to the world's coral reefs. It is indeed unique, and its geographical features and biodiversity more than justify the World Heritage status.

Kingfisher Bay Resort

Shifting Sands

The interplay of sand, wind and water shapes Fraser Island as we know it today, but this ongoing process dates back some 800,000 years. Finely eroded granite from the New England tablelands has steadily washed into the sea and moved northwards on the currents and waves swept up by the prevailing south-easterly winds. This helps explain the many beautiful beaches and sand masses along the south-east Queensland coast.

In the case of Fraser Island, sand accumulated around the rocky outcrops of Indian Head, Middle Rocks and Waddy Point – the remnants of an ancient volcano. During successive ice ages, when sea levels dropped and sand deposits dried out, the wind formed these deposits into dunes that were then colonised by plants, shrubs and trees. The sand on Fraser Island today reaches down to a depth of 30m below sea level but in places it extends as far as half a kilometre.

Happy Valley ca. 1935

JOHN OXLEY LIBRARY

Broad, sandy beaches and lightly vegetated, low foredunes of pale-brown sands characterise Fraser Island's **east coast**. Its few 'cliffs' and 'gorges' (e.g. the Pinnacles and Rainbow Gorge) are older dune deposits, compacted with silt and clay to a substance known as Teewah sand, and then eroded. Just inland are low dune ridges (30-60m above sea level) of yellow-brown sands that have been stabilised by vegetation but are still relatively young.

The **interior** of the island consists of high dune ridges (100-240m above sea level) running diagonally in a north-westerly direction and supporting dense forest. Their sands are 'layered', with leached white sand deposits over older, darker sands resting on a core of Teewah sand.

The **west coast** with its narrow beaches consists of old, white sands that are not very fertile and support stunted woodland and heath. Rolling, low-lying sand plains with many shallow lakes dominate the **north** of the island.

See Vegetation Systems, below, for more about these different environments.

Sandblows

When the dune vegetation is breached along the east coast, whether through natural causes (cyclones, fire) or human damage (trampling, fire, overgrazing), sand gets blown inland by the prevailing south-easterlies, smothering everything in its path. This is called a sandblow. As the sand marches on, sand-blasted tree trunks behind the front may be uncovered again many years later.

A sandblow often takes the form of a U-shaped "parabolic dune" cutting into and across one or more parallel dune ridges. This is the case where the sandblow's trailing arms are held back by stabilising vegetation. Where vegetation is absent or damaged, the sandblow will begin to form a new, diagonal dune ridge in the direction of the wind, usually covering an older one. Much of the island's topography has its origin in such dune ridges.

The largest sandblow on the island is the Knifeblade Sandblow near the Pinnacles, north of the wreck of the *Maheno*.

Coffee Rock

Dark, rounded 'rock' formations are visible in places along the east coast – Poyungan and Yidney rocks, for instance, or in the northern section at Ngkala Rocks. This is known as organic rock or coffee rock, which is actually sand cemented together by the fine organic colloids that have settled out of the tea-coloured water in freshwater lakes and swamps.

It is thought that these dark 'rocks' are the relics of lake beds and swamps from the last ice age, when sea levels were 120m lower than they are today and the coast was 25km further east, at the edge of the continental shelf. Fraser Island's unique perched lakes (see page 17) are only possible because they're lined with such layers of organically cemented sand.

A series of sandblows along the east coast

Freshwater Systems

The island's high inland dunes attract a lot of rain – about 1600mm a year, which is more than falls on the mainland across the strait. Strands of fungi in the sand allow the water to filter down to the underground water table (sterile sand easily repels water, believe it or not). And because sand can hold an impressive 30% of its volume in water, the island has huge reserves of freshwater.

The underground aquifer – the saturated layer of sand, the upper limit of which is the water table – is shaped like a dome or lens, with the water table rising to well above sea level in the inland areas (denser sea water holds it in place). The aquifer is believed to contain a staggering 10-20 million megalitres, of which six million megalitres are above sea level (a megalitre is a million litres, which would fill a room of 10m cubed).

To put that into perspective, Australia's total water use for irrigation purposes is 16 million megalitres a year. Australia's largest dam, the enormous Gordon Pedder dam system in Tasmania, holds almost 13 million megalitres. The contents of Sydney Harbour pale into insignificance by comparison, at half a million megalitres.

It takes 100 years or more for water in the aquifer to emerge through spring-fed creeks or lakes, or as seepage along the beach at low tide. Most creeks are on the eastern beach. Eli Creek, the best known of these, pours out 80 megalitres of water daily. But at 160 megalitres per day, Bogimbah Creek, on the west coast, is responsible for nearly half the island's daily drainage of 325 megalitres.

'Black' & 'White' Water

The water of Fraser Island's lakes and streams is described as being either black or white. 'Black' water is stained a tea colour by organic colloids (a mixture with properties between those of a solution and a fine suspension) caused by decaying reeds, plants and leaf litter, which does not affect its drinkability. 'White' water is completely clear.

The processes responsible for these differences are rather complicated. In a nutshell, water that has not gone through the water table (e.g. in impervious, low-lying swamps) tends to be black. Water that has taken many years to emerge from the water table, where aluminium acts as a catalyst to precipitate the organic ('black') colloids out, tends to be white.

Black water is highly acidic, white water is far less acidic but contains more phosphates and supports a wider variety of plant life.

'Black' water, Boomerang Lakes

Lake McKenzie, a glorious perched lake

Organic colloids settle into the sand at Boomerang Lakes, eventually forming an impervious layer of coffee rock

Lakes

It is nothing short of amazing that Fraser Island, surrounded by salt water and formed entirely by sand, has more than 50 freshwater lakes (some say 70 or even 100, depending on whether they include swamps and damp depressions that could well become fully fledged lakes over time). In Australia only Tasmania's central plateau and Victoria's western district can match such a concentration of lakes.

The island's lakes are special in many ways. Sediments in some of them date back 300,000 years, which makes them older than any other coastal lake in Australia. Some, like the perched lakes (see below), are entirely 'stand-alone', with catchment areas restricted to their immediate shores and without outlets. They contain the purest water found anywhere in the world – clean as the moment it fell out of the sky.

These lakes don't flush themselves, so they retain any contamination introduced by humans. It is vital that visitors do not use soap, shampoo, detergent, sunscreen or insect repellent of any kind in the water. The phosphates they release are particularly harmful to the natural balance of the lakes.

Most lakes are acidic (pH as low as 4.8), contain very few nutrients, and therefore support little life – the water is 'too pure'. The fish and invertebrates that manage to exist in them are often unique and distinct from lake to lake, due to the lakes' isolation from the sea and from each other.

Some frog species, appropriately called 'acid frogs', are adapted to survive in the acidic conditions. Many lakes support turtles and small, black crustaceans, along with rainbow fish. Carp gudgeon and a unique species of sunfish have also been found. Lake Wabby (the least acidic lake, with a higher level of nutrients) has no less than nine species of fish, making it the most prolific freshwater lake on the island.

Perched Lakes

The island has about 40 perched lakes, which sit in dunes well above the water table. Their base consists of coffee rock and, with one or two exceptions, they are fed entirely by rainfall.

Perched lakes are a distinguishing feature of the Great Sandy region, and Fraser Island has half the world's total. Most lakes in the high dunes on the southern half of the island are perched, including Lake McKenzie and the largest perched lake in the world, 200ha Lake Boomanjin. The Boomerang Lakes, 130m above sea level, are the world's highest.

As perched lakes are fed almost entirely by rainwater falling straight into them and in the immediate vicinity, they have very few nutrients, as well as high acidity caused by decaying organic matter, which makes them rather sterile. Most contain only one species of zooplankton, *Calamoecia tasmanica*.

Perched lakes are between three and eight metres deep and tend to have superb beaches, sometimes all the way around their shores (e.g. Basin Lake).

Window Lakes

Window lakes form where dune depressions dip below the water table, leaving a 'window' into the aquifer. They are generally found close to the coast, often in the form of swamps. All lakes in the low-lying terrain north of Orchid Beach are window lakes, including beautiful Ocean Lake.

Window lakes are shallow, less than 3m deep.

Lake Wabby, a barrage lake formed by a sandblow

Barrage Lakes

A sandblow occasionally blocks the path of a flowing creek or stream, forming a barrage lake. The only real example on Fraser Island is Lake Wabby, sandwiched between forest and the massive Hammerstone Sandblow that is encroaching at the rate of several metres a year. The wall of sand (the 'barrage') has lifted the level of the water table here.

With a depth of 11m, Lake Wabby is the deepest lake on the island, and indeed in the whole Great Sandy region. Its surface area is small but it contains the greatest variety of fish of any Fraser Island lake. The stream that feeds it may be partly responsible for this relative bounty but no-one is really sure. Pity the fish, though: in another 20 years the lake will be completely covered by sand.

Vegetation Systems

Fraser Island has a surprising variety of vegetation types, from mangrove forests and coastal heath to subtropical rainforests – it is the only place in the world where tall rainforests grow on sand dunes. Out in the Great Sandy Strait, seagrass beds extend over more than 12,500ha.

Let's take a look at different types of vegetation and the life they support, roughly from east to west across the island. For more information about specific plants and animals, see Flora & Fauna later in this chapter.

Foredunes

Plants growing on the dunes can only obtain nutrients (other than nitrogen) from rain, sea spray and what little there is in the sand itself.

Sand is coated with mineral compounds such as iron and aluminium oxides, and close to shore the air contains nutrients from sea spray which are deposited on the sand. In a symbiotic relationship, fungi in the sand make these nutrients available to the plants, turning the yellowish sand white in the process. The plants in turn supply various organic compounds to the fungi, which they cannot synthesise for themselves as they have no chlorophyll.

Salt-tolerant pioneer plants (e.g. beach spinifex) grow in this nutrient-poor soil and and in the process help stabilise the dunes. Once they establish themselves, and begin to develop nutrient layers in the sand as they die and decay, successive plant communities can grow that are also adapted to low-nutrient conditions.

Beach spinifex, the prime foredune stabiliser

These are the hardy second-colonisers such as she-oaks (casuarinas), pandanus and coastal banksias, which grow immediately behind the outer grasses and vines. Horsetail she-oaks in particular shield other plants from the ceaseless wind and salt spray, and provide shade which lowers surface temperatures and promotes moisture retention. Coastal banksias, for instance, are often found behind the first stands of she-oaks, and their flowers are a valuable food source for nectar-feeding birds and insects.

Mixed Forests

Behind the foredunes, conditions are more sheltered and nutrient layers gradually become thicker and richer. Taller, less stunted trees are able to develop, such as eucalypts (the salt-tolerant Moreton Bay ash) and acacias. Scribbly gums are a common sight, as are brush box, bloodwood, smooth-barked apple and black she-oak. Cypress pines are common in the south of the island and behind some of the mangrove areas. The understorey is dense, with bracken, foxtail ferns (actually a sedge) and blady grasses. Animals and insects are more numerous.

Further inland, forests become taller. Scribbly gums are still in evidence but forest redgum makes an appearance, along with blackbutt, tallowwood, satinay and even red mahogany.

Rainforests

Majestic, subtropical rainforests grow in the gullies of the central high dunes, where they are protected from winds and have a plentiful supply of freshwater and even greater amounts of nutrients. Competition for light is intense, which results in tall, straight-stemmed trees that have few branches until they reach the upper canopy.

The dominant trees are satinay, brush box and myrtle, while hoop and kauri pines often emerge above this 50m canopy. Down below are different types of vines, ferns and palms (especially the ubiquitous piccabeen, or bangalow, palms), along with crows nest ferns, elkhorns and occasional native orchids. The massive angiopteris fern, unchanged for millions of years, grows along creek beds and uses water pressure to support its fronds, which are the largest of any fern in the world. Fraser Island is an important habitat for many rare ferns.

Bird life is intense in these areas (cockatoos, lorikeets, parrots), various types of bats are plentiful, and the island's modest population of possums and gliders also tends to congregate here.

Right: Fraser Island's dense forest cover

Horsetail she-oaks shield other plants from the ceaseless wind

Pandanus

BRONWYN HEALING

Angiopteris ferns (here along Wanggoolba Creek), with the largest fronds in the world, date from the age of the dinosaurs

Track through a dense rainforest area

Tall piccabeen (or bangalow) palms are common

Rainforests cover about 8000ha or 5% of Fraser Island but they're mostly inaccessible except to determined hikers. The area around Central Station, and its boardwalk along crystal-clear Wanggoolba Creek, provides the easiest opportunity to marvel at this wealth of vegetation growing in sand.

Wallum Scrub & Heathlands

The western side of the island has the oldest sand deposits. Deprived of fresh layers of wind-blown sand from the south-east, the sand has been leached of its nutrients over many thousands of years and even the longest tree roots cannot reach what may be left in the deeper layers. The dense forests that once grew here have been replaced by scrub and open heathlands with shallow, spreading root systems – a retrogressive form of evolution that is quite rare.

This is wallum country, after an Aboriginal name for *Banksia aemula* (wallum banksia, with its serrated leaves), which grows on coastal lowlands with high water tables and poor soil. As is often the case with poor soils, however, the variety of vegetation is stunning with many different plant communities eking out highly specialised existences in their own little niches.

The often dense forests of banksias, stunted scribbly gums and swamp-area melaleucas alternate with open heathlands (both wet and dry) full of wildflowers that burst into colour in spring and summer, though many species also flower at other times of the year. Grass trees and a wide variety of sedges and rushes are much in evidence.

The wallum flowers attract great numbers of pollinators – birds, bats, insects – and other creatures that prey on them in turn. The area is home to several species of acid frog and other amphibians, unique freshwater fish, crustaceans and many reptiles. Wallum habitat depends on a delicate balance that is easily disturbed, but on Fraser Island it remains more or less pristine.

The wallum heathlands include a network of unique fens that are worth describing separately.

Fens

A few years after the island's World Heritage listing, ecologists were delighted to discover a complex system of peat swamps known as patterned fens inland from Moon Point, as well as in the Wathumba Swamp, at Ungowa, and near the mouths of Wanggoolba and Bogimbah creeks. Not only had these fens been unknown to science, they occurred almost at sea level and occasionally merged with mangrove forests, a combination that had not been seen anywhere else in the world.

Right: Sandy inland track through rainforest

PHOTO: ROB BOEGHEIM

Patterned fens usually exist at high altitudes and latitudes (Scotland, Siberia, Scandinavia, Canada, Tasmania and alpine regions of New Zealand) and are formed by melting snow and ice in association with mossy vegetation. The discovery of Fraser Island's fens adds a new dimension to this theory.

Fens are based on very slowly decaying plant material, which at a certain point becomes peat. Differing rates of peat formation in fens can create 'string' patterns of pools, streams and ridges. However, in another world first, some of Fraser Island's fens show reticulated, 'leopard' patterns that have so far only been

found in bogs. A bog is self-growing in its own water supply whereas a fen has water flowing through it. Both fen types exist side by side at Moon Point.

Scientists believe that Fraser Island's fens may be the oldest in the world and that their preservative peat holds a unique record of environmental change over many thousands of years (see "History in the Fens"). So far the only fens found elsewhere in Australia are in Cooloola, which has a similar environment, and in Tasmania.

The fens provide an important habitat for endangered species such as ground parrots, false water rats and acid frogs.

history in the fens

ANGUS TYE, a student working on his doctoral thesis at the University of Melbourne's School of Anthropology, Geography and Environmental Studies, has been taking core samples from fens on the island to find out more about its pre-European history. He is particularly interested in the effects of fire management by the original inhabitants. Here's his story:

Fraser Island and the other sand islands that make up this coastline of south-east Queensland have been kicking on for a long, long time. My research concentrates on a small fragment of this time, just 10,000 years. Ten-thousand years ago, towards the end of the last ice age, all of these sand islands were joined to the mainland and to each other, due to water bound up in glaciers, ice caps and snow around the world. As these melted, the islands became separated.

The current theory is that as you travel across the islands from east to west the soil (sand) gets older and therefore has fewer nutrients available to the plants. The different plants that you see as you travel from one side to the other are a result of these differing levels of nutrients.

How does this work exactly? Well, as the age of the soil increases, the layer at which the nutrients are located lies deeper and deeper. On the west coast of Fraser Island, in the wallum heathlands, this can be 20m below the surface, far too deep for plant roots to access. In addition, the plants that inhabit these older

landscapes do not produce as much litter to compensate for the leaching of nutrients.

This is where the indigenous use of fire helped maintain a delicate balance. Burning vegetation and releasing the nutrients to the soil in the form of ash recharged the system. The interval of these fires was crucial to providing fresh nutrients for the plants.

What is of interest is how these islands have developed in the last 10,000 years. Has the use of fire made a difference? By wading around in swamps, digging holes and outrunning dingoes, I am trying to work this story out. I do this by taking cores of sediment from swamps and then analysing the pollen and charcoal that has fallen into that particular swamp over time.

I hope to find out how the sand islands in this region have developed since they were isolated 10,000 years ago. Can we use this theory of decreasing nutrients as a broadscale approach to land classification? Are they developing in the same direction, or are they evolving differently due to different burning regimes? Why are there no rainforests on North Stradbroke Island? Areas such as rainforests have depended heavily on the absence of fire, whereas the open eucalypt forests and wallum heathlands have depended heavily on the regular presence of fire. What approach to management in the future is best suited to maintaining this amazing environment?

I hope to establish what the landscape was like when the Butchulla people lived with the land, and how their use of fire shaped it.

Mangrove Forests

Wallum scrub and heathland runs right up to the western beach but it can also merge with mangrove forests, which are common in the intertidal estuaries, inlets and bays. Often dismissed as inhospitable and dangerous swamps with hip-deep mud, ridden with mosquitoes and sand flies, mangroves form a productive ecosystem with several important functions.

They protect coastal land by controlling erosion and stabilising sediment, and also act as a natural purifier of coastal water by trapping and filtering out pollution. They serve as a bridging ecosystem between freshwater and marine systems, and as such are vital nurseries and feeding grounds for hundreds of species including fish, crabs, birds and bats.

A good way to appreciate the intricacy and wealth of mangrove forests is to explore them by dinghy or canoe on the incoming tide.

Flora & Fauna

Fraser Island's different habitats are home to an amazing variety of plants and animals, some of which are unique to this environment. It would be beyond the scope of this book to deal with them all, and some have already been mentioned above. This section describes a few of the more common or noteworthy species.

Flora

The island has at least six major plant communities and almost 800 species and subspecies, from spiky coastal flora to lush rainforest vegetation. Plants include three species listed as endangered, four as vulnerable and nine as rare. A few, such as the bright-pink *Drosera lovellae*, the largest of the carnivorous sundews, grow only on Fraser Island.

Common Trees & Shrubs

A common sight is the **scribbly gum** (*Eucalyptus racemosa*) with strange 'scribbles' all over its trunk. These are made by the hungry larvae of scribbly gum moths (*Ogmograptis scribula*) and are only found on these trees and on the high, smooth parts of **blackbutt** trees (*Eucalyptus pilularis*), which are also common with their dark, rough lower trunks.

Another eucalypt often found on the eastern side of the island is the **Moreton Bay ash** or carbeen (*Corymbia tessellaris*), the most salt-resistant of the eucalypts and well adapted to this environment. Hardy **she-oaks** (*Allocasuarina* and *Casuarina* spp.) grow in abundance on the sand dunes of the eastern beach facing the wind and salt spray, but are also common throughout the island with their thin, drooping branchlets and hard, woody cones. She-oaks are known as nitrogen fixers and add precious nutrients to the soil.

Behind the first stands of coastal she-oaks are **banksias** (*Banksia* spp.), a fast-growing group of Australian plants with hardy, leathery leaves and large, spiky flowers that develop into woody fruits which contain seeds. They're common understorey plants throughout the island, along with various **wattle, tea-tree** and **geebung** species (*Acacia, Leptospermum/Melaleuca* and *Persoonia* spp.). Paperbark tea trees (*Melaleuca quinquenervia*) grow as sprawling, 1-2m shrubs in exposed dune areas where the wind twists them into bizarre shapes, but they can reach 25m in sheltered areas. In low-lying, swampy ground, paperbarks often thrive to the exclusion of other trees.

Another common understorey plant on both the eastern and western sides of the island is the bright-green **foxtail fern** (*Caustis blakei*), which is actually a sedge and in many instances replaces the grasses. Then there are the burrawang or **zamia palms** (*Macrozamia douglasii*), close relatives of prehistoric cycads and also nitrogen fixers, and Australia's famous **grass trees** (*Xanthorrhoea* spp.). The spear-like stems of grass trees can be well over a metre in length and are covered in hundreds of tiny, nectar-filled flowers that make way for woody seed capsules.

ROB BOEGHEIM

Banksia flowers develop into woody fruits containing the seeds

Foxtail ferns

The furrowed bark of the satinay

Roadside satinays

Tall Trees

The island's tallest trees grow in the rainforest pockets and in the drier, tall forests that surround these. The majestic **satinay** (*Syncarpia hillii*), also known as Fraser Island turpentine, is rarely found outside the Great Sandy region. It has a rough, deeply furrowed bark, and grows to over 40m with a girth of more than 4m. Its timber is resistant to marine borers – Pile Valley (which has some fine satinays) is so named because satinay piles were used to refurbish the Suez Canal and London's docks.

Pile Valley also has good examples of another giant, the **brush box** (*Lophostemon confertus*), also known as **pink box** or **Queensland box**, with its tessellated ('tiled') bark and smooth, pinkish limbs. In dry forest areas it may only grow to around 10m but here it can attain heights of well over 30m. Its timber has a luscious shine and was often used for floor boards.

Other tall hardwoods include **blackbutt** (very common around Lake McKenzie) and **tallowwood** (*Eucalyptus microcorys*), a native rainforest eucalypt that was used in house-building for floorboards and exposed beams.

Notable softwoods include the magnificent **kauri pine** (*Agathis robusta*), a tall, native pine that was heavily logged for panelling and furniture. Few examples of mature stands exist today, though some still grow in the Yidney Scrub. Another tall native, the **hoop pine** (*Araucaria cunninghamii*) with its distinctive, raised rings along the trunk, was also heavily logged. A few fine specimens can be seen around Central Station.

Foredune Pioneers

The most common sand-colonising plant on the seaward slopes of dunes is the **sand** or **beach spinifex** (*Spinifex sericeus*). This stout grass produces long, creeping runners that grow roots and new, leafy branches from nodes along the runners. These reduce wind velocity along the dune surface and encourage new sand deposits, making spinifex essential to foredune formation and stabilisation.

Another salt-tolerant, primary coloniser is the **sea purslane** (*Sesuvium portula-castrum*). This succulent herb also produces creepers, with smallish, purple or pink flowers at the stems of its leaves. Unlike spinifex, it doesn't survive burial under sand and favours slightly more sheltered foredune. The **beach primrose** (*Oenothera drummondii*) with its bright-yellow, four-petalled flowers also prefers a bit of shelter.

FRANK STOFFELS

Central Station

Beach spinifex, with creeping runners

Other common creepers include the introduced **dune morning glory** (*Ipomoea indica*) with beautiful, trumpet-shaped flowers; the **goat's foot** (*Ipomoea pes-caprae*) with large, goatfoot-shaped leaves and pink, bell-shaped flowers in spring; and not to forget the ubiquitous **pigface** (*Carpobrotus glaucescens*) with its thick, fleshy foliage and purple flowers.

Pigface in flower

Wallum Scrub & Heathlands

The poor soils on the western side of the island are home to an amazing variety of flowering plants. **Wide Bay boronia** (*Boronia rivularis*) is thought to exist only in the Great Sandy region. It has a seasonal abundance of waxy, purple flowers, and is common in the wetter areas. The mauve-flowered **forest boronia** (*Boronia rosmarinifolia*) with its scented leaves is more common in open forests.

The ubiquitous, lemon-scented **tea trees** (*Leptospermum* spp.) also have highly scented leaves. Their waxy, white flowers develop into woody seed cases.

In August and September, **wedding bush** (*Ricinocarpus pinifolius*) is covered in a profusion of small, five-petalled, white flowers. There are a number of **pea-flowers** (*Fabaceae* family), most of which are yellow in colour, plus a number of **small-leaved heaths** (*Epacridaceae* family) that flower at various times throughout the year, giving visitors a display of wildflowers virtually all year round.

Vegetation also includes three types of banksia (*Banksia aemula, B. robur* and *B. integrifolia*), grass trees, she-oaks, (small) Fraser Island satinay, brush box, pink bloodwood (*Corymbia intermedia*), cypress pines (*Callitris columellaris*) and a number of sedges and rushes (*Restionaceae* and *Cyperacea* families).

Common heath (Epacris obtusifolia) in bloom

Mangroves

Mangrove trees are readily identifiable by their above-ground roots (pneumatophores) which help to provide oxygen to the tree. Twelve varieties exist in the area, the most common being the river, grey and yellow mangroves.

Different mangrove species often have different root types. For example, the grey mangrove (*Avicennia marina*) has short, straight pneumatophores that stick out of the mud. The stilted or red mangrove (*Rhizophora stylosa*) has branching pneumatophores that form an above-ground network of stabilising prop roots, a habitat for mud crabs.

Dense mangrove forest

The adaptable swamp oak (*Casuarina glauca*), the most salt-tolerant of the she-oaks, often grows at the edges of mangrove forests.

Weeds

About 7% of Fraser Island's plant species are introduced, which is a low percentage. Some, such as umbrella trees, are native on the mainland and have been relatively benign so far on the island, but others have become a serious problem.

fireweed

Anyone having fun along the eastern beach (fishers in particular) should beware of a stinging, dark-reddish growth known as fireweed. It causes stinging within minutes to hours after direct contact, which can develop into blistering. Contact with the eye, nose and mouth regions can cause severe swelling. Medical attention may be required.

The culprit is a blue-green alga called *Lyngbya majuscula*, which attaches itself to seagrass, seaweed and rocks, and grows in clumps or mats of fine, cotton wool-like strands 10-30cm long. Large mats can float to the surface and wash up on the beach, often mixed with seagrass.

It is also known as mermaid hair and stinging limu. Fraser Islanders refer to it as fireweed, which can be confusing because that's also the name of a stinging hydroid commonly found in south-east Queensland waters.

Scientists are still trying to work out what causes *Lyngbya* blooms, but they do know that northerly winds can bring floating weed inshore and onto the beach, whereas the prevailing south-easterlies tend to carry it out to sea.

Don't swim or wade in areas where *Lyngbya* is growing or floating in the water, and don't touch material washed onto the beach. The EPA issues fireweed warnings during danger periods. More information is available at the ranger stations on the island.

beware

These include groundsel along the west coast and lantana in pockets throughout, both of which form impenetrable thickets. Notoriously hardy plants such as bitou bush, asparagus ferns and sisal have also gained a foothold.

Some weeds have been introduced by birds or by the wind, but others such as umbrella and sisal trees have been intentionally planted by humans in the past century.

Visitors can unwittingly bring weeds onto the island or spread them around, so it's always a good idea to check for seeds or pieces of plant on shoes, socks, clothing and cars. Car tyres are believed to have introduced the devastating *Phytophthera cinnamomi* soil fungus to many Australian parks, though so far not to Fraser Island.

Fauna

Fraser Island has a smaller variety of animals than the mainland, but thanks to the island's location at the southern or northern limit of some species, there's an interesting mix of fauna seldom found elsewhere. Apart from birds and dingoes, they can be hard to spot as they are small and often nocturnal. Scientists are still discovering new species, such as the reduced limb skink (*Coggeria naufragus*), a 'sand swimmer' that was entirely new to science but turned out to be quite common on the island.

Each animal has a place, be it as a predator or pollinator, soil enricher or seed carrier. Disturbing even the smallest animal can disrupt this delicate environmental balance.

Dingoes

When the topic of conversation turns to Fraser Island wildlife it's usually about dingoes. The most famous of the island's 30 mammal species has a reputation far in excess of its actual numbers (160-300 depending on breeding conditions and natural selection processes).

Dingoes hit the news headlines several years ago when a child died from bites received while holidaying on the island. In response, the government culled the more troublesome dingoes but resisted calls to wipe out the entire population.

The dingo (*Canis lupus dingo*) arrived in Australia 3000-8000 years ago and has been here long enough to be considered a native animal. It is similar to the domestic dog and the two can interbreed, which poses the main threat to its survival as a pure strain. However, unlike domestic dogs, dingoes only have one litter of three to four pups a year, usually around

August/September. They're territorial, live in small packs and often howl in chorus, similar to wolves and coyotes.

Thanks to Fraser Island's isolation from the mainland and the (now) total ban on domestic dogs, its dingoes represent the purest strain in Australia. The population is large enough to prevent inbreeding and isolated enough to prevent crossbreeding – only 17% are hybrids. An outbreak of canine parvovirus introduced by domestic dogs in the late 1970s had a devastating effect on their numbers.

They feed on birds and small mammals such as rats and bandicoots, and in their natural state they're a very lean animal, almost like a greyhound. They are not natural scavengers, though such behaviour has been encouraged by thoughtless people.

Dingoes have a natural fear of humans, but some people have treated dingoes like the friendly family dog, by feeding and encouraging them to come close. They are not like the domesticated family dog – they are wild and deserve the same respect we show to all other wild, carnivorous animals.

It is vital for the success and health of the dingo population, as well as personal safety, that they are not fed. It is also imperative that small children do not become separated from

KINGFISHER BAY RESORT

Dingoes are wild animals. Problems arise when visitors treat them like the friendly family dog

their parents, and the government strongly recommends that campers with children aged under 14 use the fenced campgrounds at Central Station, Lake Boomanjin, Dilli Village and Waddy Point.

Vigilance is always required as dingoes' behaviour can be most unpredictable. They are more boisterous, curious and territorial from January to May when young males are fighting for dominance and territory during breeding.

Bats

Bats, or *Chiroptera* (from 'chiro', hand, and 'pteron', wing), are the only mammals to have mastered true flight. They are the most common mammal on the island, comprising almost half the mammal species recorded here.

These nocturnal creatures can be divided into two groups – the **flying foxes** (or fruit bats), which rely on sight and smell to locate the fruits and blossoms of trees and shrubs such as eucalypts and banksias; and the insectivorous **microbats,** which use echolocation (sonar) to catch insects on the wing.

Flying foxes commute nightly to Fraser Island from daytime roosts, called camps, at Hervey Bay and the mouth of the Mary River on the mainland, though some also form temporary camps on the island in the mangroves and rainforest. The most common species here is the **grey-headed flying fox** (*Pteropus poliocephalus*), a noisy feeder with a wingspan of 120-160cm. Another species is the **black flying fox** (*Pteropus alecto*), the largest Australian fruit bat, with a wingspan of up to 180cm. The island also has the smallest fruit bat, the **Queensland blossom bat** (*Syconycteris australis*), with a wingspan of 25cm. It roosts in dense foliage and feeds on nectar from native trees, often hovering to do so.

Microbats consume half their body weight in insects nightly. They roost in tree hollows on the island, though two species are cave dwellers – and as Fraser Island has no caves, it is believed that some may commute from as far away as Gympie. A common tree dweller here is the **little broad-nosed bat** (*Scotorepens greyii*), with a wingspan of 20-26cm, which feeds in forest gaps. Cave dwellers include the common **bentwing bat** (*Miniopterus schreibersii*), with a wingspan of 27-34cm.

Microbats tend to be seen and not heard, as their echolocation pulses are usually well above the frequencies that humans can hear. One exception is the **white-striped mastiff bat**

Be Dingo Aware

In their natural state, dingoes are hunters, not scavengers. But they're intelligent animals and if humans present them with an easy feed, they'll go for it and in the process lose their hunting skills. The only way to preserve their natural lifestyle is to decrease their reliance on humans, which will also restore their natural shyness and decrease the likelihood of aggressive behaviour.

Dingoes can open iceboxes, so lock or strap your iceboxes securely or store them in your vehicle. Make sure you store food and rubbish in locked containers or in your vehicle, otherwise it's an open invitation. Dingoes will sneak food from bait buckets, grab rubbish bags from tents, and dig up fish offal and toilet waste along the beach if it's not buried deep enough. They may even rip open tents – even if there's no food inside. Put your belongings in your vehicle when you're away from your campsite so dingoes can see there is nothing of interest inside the tent.

- **Stay with your children at all times** – younger dingoes practise dominating behaviour on children. Adults have also been attacked, so walk in groups or carry a stick when walking alone.

- **Do not encourage or coax dingoes to come closer for a photo.** Keep your distance and watch them quietly. Dingoes can read attention-getting antics as a signal to become threatening.

- **Never feed dingoes, even indirectly.** Lock up your food stores and iceboxes, and pack away your food scraps and rubbish.

- **If you feel threatened by a dingo, stand still at your full height, face the dingo, calmly back away and confidently call another adult.** Don't run or wave your arms.

- **If attacked, defend yourself aggressively.** Strike the dingo with an object such as a stick, backpack or coat.

Report any negative encounter with dingoes to the next ranger you see. Take note of identifying features, such as ear tags (males in the left ear, females in the right) and any distinctive markings (white leg 'socks', other fur patterns, injuries etc).

Remember: it's illegal to feed or leave food available for dingoes or disturb them in any way. Penalties up to $3000 apply, with on-the-spot fines of $225. Dingoes may look hungry or starved, but they're naturally lean and looking for an easy meal.

A regularly updated *Be Dingo-Aware!* brochure is provided with your vehicle or camping permit. Read this vital information – it may help avoid a tragedy and can save you money.

(*Tadarida australis*), which emits an audible call at 13kHz. It's the largest microbat with a wingspan of 41-45cm, and can be seen in fast, direct flight above the canopy.

Other Terrestrial Mammals

Fraser Island is poor grazing country so there are no kangaroos, though there's a small population of swamp wallabies. Koalas were probably hunted out by Aborigines. Bandicoots and short-beaked echidnas exist here quite successfully, however, digging around in the loose sand for insects, worms and roots.

Sugar gliders (*Petaurus breviceps*) and squirrel gliders (*Petaurus norfolcensis*) can sometimes be spotted at night gliding between branches among the tree tops in search of nectar and insects. **Feathertail gliders** (*Acrobates pygmaeus*) live on the island too, but can be difficult to observe due to their tiny size and are easily mistaken for a gliding leaf.

Rodents also do quite well in this environment, with nine native species. The abundant, attractively pale-coloured **pale field rat** (*Rattus tunneyi*) lives off grass stems, seeds and roots. The **native bush rat** (*Rattus fuscipes*) is also common, feeding on insects and vegetation. Both are nocturnal. One of the few native rodents that also hunts during the day, often at sunset, is the **web-footed water rat** (*Hydromys* *chrysogaster*), which lives near permanent bodies of water where it feeds on aquatic insects, crustaceans, fish and the occasional water bird.

Rather than burrow and nest underground, the **grassland melomys** (*Melomys burtoni*) constructs a conical nest from shredded leaves woven around grass or other slim plant stalks. The **fawn-footed melomys** (*Melomys cervinipes*) is an excellent climber and is usually found in forest areas.

The **yellow-footed antechinus** (*Antechinus flavipes*) is a carnivorous marsupial that turns its prey inside out, feasting on the insides. It mates aggressively – biting, scratching and copulating for up to 12 hours. This causes extreme stress to the male, leading to a breakdown of the immune system and death, which protects the young from competition from adult males.

There are still a few wild horses, or **brumbies**, around Orchid Beach, descended from domestic horses introduced in the 1800s. In the 1930s there were about 2000 brumbies on the island, but they were gradually shot out and eventually culled completely in 1987 – or so it was thought.

A couple of years later several brumbies wandered out of the bush into the Orchid Beach area, where they have been left to roam. The EPA classes them as feral because they cause environmental damage to the foredunes, and occasionally lash out at humans who get too close, and has decided to remove them to the mainland. This is not without controversy, however, as some Butchulla elders want them to remain.

Birds

Birds are the most abundant fauna on the island. Almost half of Australia's 750 bird species have been sighted here (354 to date, and counting). Oddly, there are no emus or bush turkeys even though this habitat would suit them well – it is believed that the Aborigines hunted them to extinction.

The island is an important stop-over site for wading birds, which rest here during their long flights to/from breeding grounds in Siberia. Many are subject to international protection treaties. The largest migratory wader, the **eastern curlew** (*Numenius madagascariensis*), can be seen from August to March. **Whimbrels** (*Numenius phaeopus*) hang around from September to April. A resident wader, the **pied oystercatcher** (*Haematopus longirostris*), can often be seen at low tide looking for **pippis** (bivalve molluscs).

Some of the island's birds are rare or vulnerable. The **ground parrot** (*Pezoporus wallicus*) is one of the rarest and least commonly sighted – people have been known literally to step on them. This green and yellow, ground-dwelling bird lives among coastal sedges in the wallum heathlands and constructs a nest at or near ground level from surrounding vegetation.

Red and green **king parrots** (*Alisterus scapularis*) can be seen eating nuts, berries and fruits. Other brightly coloured parrots and lorikeets feeding on nectar or blossoms high among the tree tops are the gregarious **rainbow lorikeets** (*Trichoglossus haematodus*) and the **scaly-breasted lorikeets** (*Trichoglossus chlorolepidotus*).

Nectar-feeding birds with their long, thin, curved beaks include the **white-cheeked honeyeaters** (*Phylidonyris nigra*), **Lewin's honeyeaters** (*Meliphaga lewinii*) and the smallest of the honeyeaters, the richly coloured **scarlet honeyeaters** (*Myzomela sanguinolenta*).

The male **grey shrike-thrush** (*Colluricincla harmonica*) develops a beautiful song voice

Birds are the island's most abundant fauna.

ROB BOEGHEIM

Plovers

during the breeding season from August to December. The male **mistletoe bird** (*Dicaeum hirundinaceum*) also has a distinctive, clear song. This tiny, glossy, blue-black and scarlet bird can be seen among mistletoe plants.

Tiny **red-backed fairy-wrens** (*Malurus melanocephalus*) move quickly through the dense tea tree shrubs and surrounding bush. During the breeding season from August to February, the male develops prominent red and black plumage to attract his mate who retains a plainer brown plumage all year.

Several kingfishers nest and breed on the island. The largest, the **laughing kookaburra** (*Dacelo novaeguineae*), lacks the brilliant blues of the smaller **forest kingfisher** (*Halcyon macleayi*), or the green of the **sacred kingfisher** (*Halcyon sancta*). The forest and sacred kingfishers are migratory, and in summer they make nests in termite mounds in trees. The **azure kingfisher** (*Ceyx azurea*) has a rich, glossy blue plumage on its back and sides and an orange or buff-coloured chest. This small bird appears full of character as it sits on low-hanging branches

or roots, giving out a distinctive, shrill squeak before darting off to catch a small fish.

Sometimes mistaken for a kingfisher is the **rainbow bee-eater** (*Merops ornatus*), whose colours become iridescent as the sun catches them. They catch insects on the wing, including bees and wasps, returning to their perch to remove the sting before swallowing them. They make their nests by tunnelling into sand dunes and creek banks.

The whip-like call of the **eastern whipbird** (*Psophodes olivaceus*) is often the only sign of this secretive bird, as it spends most of its time camouflaged among fallen logs and leaves looking for insects. Also difficult to see is the **brown quail** (*Coturnix australis*), as it blends in with the banksia thickets in the wallum heathlands where it searches for insects and seeds.

Nocturnal birds, such as **tawny frogmouths** (*Podargus strigoides*) and **owls** (*Tyto* spp.), are sometimes observed at night, swooping silently down from the trees to catch prey. During the day, the frogmouth roosts on branches and looks like a dead stump with its mottled grey and brown plumage.

Fraser Island is home to no less than 18 species of raptors. One of the largest is the **white-breasted sea eagle** (*Haliaeetus leucogaster*), which has a wingspan of two metres or more. **Brahminy kites** (*Haliastur indus*) are also common, with their distinctive and contrasting chestnut-brown and white feathers. The **osprey** (*Pandion haliaetus*), also known as the fish-hawk, uses its talons to snatch prey from the water. Osprey numbers are declining on the mainland because of river pollution by toxic pesticides, but they are quite common on the island.

You'll often see sea birds diving into the ocean after fish, such as **brown boobies** (*Sula dactylatra*) and **Australasian gannets** (*Morus serrator*). **Cormorants** (*Phalacrocorax* spp.) and **darters** (*Anhinga melanogaster*) dry their wings on yacht masts and branches.

See also Bird-Watching in the What to Do chapter.

Brahminy kite

There are more than 60 species of reptiles on the island.

Reptiles

There are more than 60 species of reptiles on the island, the largest of which, the **lace monitor** (*Varanus varius*), is frequently observed scavenging around camping areas. The most commonly encountered lizards are **skinks** (*family Scincidae*), including some very rare species. The smaller species feed primarily on insects, the larger ones are omnivorous.

There's also a wide range of venomous and nonvenomous **snakes**. Most visitors will never see a snake because they are shy creatures who prefer to hide – occasionally you may see a python moving slowly through the vegetation or sunning itself on a warm track. Even so, when bushwalking it's advisable to wear boots, socks and long, heavyweight trousers. Tramp heavily and snakes will usually slither away before you come near. *Always* leave snakes alone.

Nonvenomous snakes include the **green tree snake** *(Dendrelaphis punctulata)*, which varies in colour from olive green to grey along the back with a lemon-yellow belly; and the **eastern small-blotched python** (*Morelia maculosus*). Even though these snakes are non venomous they can still bite if provoked.

The island's four venomous snake species are the **death adder** (*Acanthophis antarcticus*), the **taipan** (*Oxyuranus scutellatus*), the **eastern brown snake** (*Pseudonaja textilis*) and the **red-bellied black snake** (*Pseudechis porphyriacus*), with its glossy, black back, bright-red sides and red underbelly. It is thought that the recent arrival of cane toads (see next page) has had a devastating effect on the death-adder population.

Short-necked turtles in Lake Allom

FRANK STOFFELS

Freshwater Turtles

The freshwater lakes are home to the **Krefft's river turtle** (*Emydura krefftii*), which has a conspicuous, pale-yellow streak along the side of its head. Scientists are still unsure whether the island version of this turtle, also called the Fraser Island short-necked turtle, should be accorded a separate status. It differs slightly from the mainland version (it's darker in colour and smaller in size), but that could have more to do with environmental factors than genetic differences.

It's omnivorous, feeding on sedge shoots, algae, insect larvae and crustaceans. Interestingly, the tea-coloured ('black-water') lakes have larger populations of these turtles than clear-water lakes such as Lake McKenzie but those in the latter are healthier and fatter.

Marine Turtles

Several species of marine turtle breed on the north-west beach between Rooney Point and Sandy Cape, often hundreds at a time. Some only come to these waters to mate in October/November and then lay their eggs on the Barrier Reef islands further north. These include the endangered **loggerhead turtle** (*Caretta caretta*), though some loggerheads also come ashore to lay eggs between October and May.

Frogs

There are 17 different species of frog on the island. These include tree, sedge, rocket and southern frogs. Of special interest are four 'acid frogs' – the Cooloola sedge frog, wallum rocket frog, wallum sedge frog and wallum froglet. They have adapted to the low pH (high acidity) levels of most lakes and swamps on the island, and are abundant in the wallum heathlands that are avoided by the more alkaline species of frog.

The **Cooloola sedge frog** (*Litoria cooloolensis*) is a small, rare frog found only on Fraser Island and in the Cooloola region. The **wallum rocket frog** (*Litoria freycineti*) is aptly named as it is able to jump more than two metres. The **emerald-spotted tree frog** (*Litoria peronii*), which has emerald-green spots on its back and a long, loud call, lives a little further back from the swamp edge, often on melaleuca trees.

The well camouflaged **copper-backed brood-frog** (*Pseudophryne raveni*) and the **wallum froglet** (*Crinia tinnule*) are hard to find, in contrast to the **striped marsh** frog (*Limnodynastes peronii*), **green tree frog** (*Litoria caerulea*) and **striped rocket frog** (*Litoria nasuta*).

Frogs are 'bio-indicators', which means they are sensitive to environmental changes and are one of the first groups of animals to disappear from a disrupted area. Native frogs are also under threat from **cane toads** (*Bufo marinus*), which have made their way onto the island in recent years, though so far their numbers are limited.

Invertebrates

Many of the island's invertebrates have special adaptations to the sandy environment and are found only at Fraser Island and Cooloola. Some 'swim' through the soft sand, such as the **burrowing cockroaches** (*Geoscapheus* spp.), which feed on dry leaf litter. They include the 8cm *Geoscapheus primulatus*, the second-largest cockroach in the world.

Several specialised cricket species 'swim' through the sand as well. One of the more interesting is the appropriately named **Cooloola monster** (*Cooloola propator*), a honey-coloured carnivore that was discovered in 1976. It resembles a cricket and is clearly an orthopteran (the order of crickets, locusts and grasshoppers), but its sperm is the most primitive of any orthopteran and it has been placed in its own suborder called Cooloolidae.

Earthworms tend to avoid sand but Fraser Island has several unique species that have adapted to this environment, including the 80cm **giant earthworm** (*Digaster keasti*). **Ants** are happy in sand and a staggering 300-plus species have been recorded in the Great Sandy region. **Termites** are also plentiful.

The island has its share of stinging insects (see "Flying Stingers"), but Fraser's **native bees** (*order Hymenoptera*) don't sting. These important pollinators are about half the size of the common bee and collect nectar from flowering native plants. They live in hives in logs and on trees.

Spiders thrive here too, from rainforest to heath, with some spectacular examples including graceful orb weavers and terrifying huntsmen, redbacks and funnel-webs. You don't often come across the dangerous ones but it pays to be careful when bushwalking. Seek immediate medical attention when bitten – the funnel-webs here are reputed to be the most lethal spiders on earth. They're prevalent in mossy banks and decaying logs.

The **bird-eating spider** (*Selenocosmia crassipes*), also known as the barking or whistling spider, is the size of a human hand. When disturbed, it 'barks' or 'whistles' by rubbing its palps with its fangs.

Backgrounds

flying stingers

Sand Flies

The intertidal estuaries and mangroves along the west coast are prime habitats for highly irritating sand flies. Also known as sand fleas, biting gnats and 'no-see-ums', these beige-coloured insects are more correctly referred to as biting midges.

They belong to the fly family of *Ceratopogonidae*, only a few groups of which are known to bite in order to suck blood. Only the females do this, to procure protein for egg development (the males, like the females, feed on plant saps and nectar).

Due to their tiny size – often no more than 0.5mm – they are virtually invisible, and because their bites may not begin itching until a few hours later, most people don't realise they've been bitten until it's too late to prevent further attacks. The next day the itching can become annoying to almost unbearable, and the bites begin to show up as red marks and even chickenpox-type blisters that can last for days or even weeks.

Reactions are most severe among people who have just arrived in the area. The body seems to build up some immunity over time, and local residents are far less affected. Fortunately, biting midges are not known to transmit diseases in Australia, although persistent scratching can cause secondary infections in the affected areas.

Prevention & Treatment

The critters rest at night like other flies and are most active around dusk and dawn (they bury themselves in the sand during the heat of day). Windy weather will keep them at bay because their capacity for flight is limited – which is why they are rarely a problem along the eastern beach with its prevailing south-easterlies. Some anglers say that fishing is best when sand flies are biting fiercely.

To avoid being bitten, wear loose-fitting clothing (they can bite through thin fabric) and apply a repellent to exposed skin. Lotions containing 20-35% DEET (diethyl toluamide) appear to be very effective (higher concentrations don't work better), but DEET is not recommended for those with sensitive skin or for children under the age of six. Alternatives are citronella or tea tree oil, and as the midges can't handle oil, any oily lotion should work

(try a mixture of dettol and baby oil in a spray bottle). Some people swear that eating garlic and/or vitamin B makes the skin unpalatable to most biting insects.

Anti-itching lotions will help soothe the irritation and reduce swelling, as will tea tree oil, rubbing alcohol or even straight vodka or gin. Calamine lotion or a plaster made from baking soda and water draw out the toxins. In very severe cases, medical treatment with antihistamines may be required.

March Flies

March flies belong to the Tabanidae family and inhabit moist forests, woodlands and swamps – anywhere near water.

Like sand flies, only the females suck blood. Unlike sand flies, however, which pierce skin with a hypodermic proboscis, female tabanids have two large, blade-like mouth parts with which they slash the skin. This creates a large and painful puncture site that oozes blood, which is then lapped up. Due to the large amount of anti-coagulant saliva involved, the wound will continue to bleed long after the fly has departed.

Tabanids are most active in the warmer months, but like sand flies, they rest at night. Fortunately they are slow fliers and hover before landing on their victim, so they are easily swatted. They see in ultra-violet and seem to prefer dark-blue colours, so light-coloured clothing may help to deter them somewhat. Insect repellent containing DEET (see Prevention & Treatment, above) is also effective.

March flies are not known to transmit diseases in Australia, and their painful bites very rarely cause allergic reactions.

Mosquitoes

Mosquitoes can be a real problem on the west coast, especially at dusk when they are most active, and they will keep many an unprepared camper awake at night as well. Like sand flies, they can also be a problem on the east coast when there is a prolonged period of wind from the north or northwest. Come prepared with all the usual repellents, long sleeves and pants, and well-shielded sleeping areas.

Mosquitoes are less of a problem in the cooler months.

Whales & Dolphins

Many marine mammals visit the waters around Fraser Island. **Minke whales** (*Balaenoptera acutorostrata*) often swim past on their own or in small groups. The **bottlenose dolphin** (*Tursiops truncatus*), **common dolphin** (*Delphinus delphis*) and **Indo-Pacific humpback dolphin** (*Sousa chinensis*) are widespread in the area, while the **Risso's dolphin** (*Grampus griseus*) makes an occasional appearance. The most famous mammal in these waters, however, would have to be the humpback whale.

Humpback Whales

Humpbacks are a huge attraction off Fraser Island in more ways than one. Every autumn, pods of them migrate 6000km from their rich feeding grounds in the Antarctic to the (sub)tropical coastal waters off eastern and western Australia to breed and give birth. (Interestingly, the eastern and western groups rarely mix down south.) Indian Head is a good viewing point at this time of year.

Between August and October, they move south again with their newborn calves, and some of them enter Hervey Bay where they spend a few days before continuing their journey back to the Antarctic. This makes the bay one of the best areas in the world to view these magnificent creatures up close – see Whale-Watching p97 for further details.

It's not clear why they enter the bay because they don't do it on their journey north. A popular theory is that Fraser Island and Breaksea Spit act as a 'scoop' that traps them – they can't continue through the shallow southern exit and have to swim north again around the island. But perhaps Hervey Bay also presents a convenient resting area before they tackle the open South Pacific Ocean.

The official name for humpbacks is *Megaptera novaeangliae*, or 'New England big-wing', for their huge, wing-like pectoral fins or flippers that can be 5m long. Their popular name derives from the way they arch their back when they begin a deep dive.

An estimated 10,000 humpbacks live in the northern hemisphere, where they make similar migrations from the Arctic to warmer breeding areas, while about 8000 inhabit the southern oceans. Some 5000 of these breed in Australian waters, and those that migrate along the eastern Australian coast are thought to represent half that number. Pods range in size from two to 15 and usually consist of mothers and calves escorted by an adult male, though the first pods migrating south in August may not yet include calves.

Humpbacks are black or dark grey on top, in striking contrast to the white underneath. Their tails, or flukes, have black patterns on the underside that are as individually unique as fingerprints are to us. Their heads have wart-like lumps called tubercles, which no other whales have. Each tubercle has a long hair growing from the centre, possibly a sensing device for the humpbacks' primary food source of krill.

KINGFISHER BAY RESORT

Humpback breaching

A humpback performs a pectoral slap while another spy hops

KINGFISHER BAY RESORT

Females are slightly bigger than males, and mature ones can grow to 15m and weigh 40 tonnes (including half a tonne of barnacles!). This makes them the fifth-largest whale species, half the size and a third of the weight of the 30m blue whale.

In spite of their bulk, humpbacks are impressive acrobats and their behaviour on the surface can be delightful. It's tempting to believe that they do this out of sheer playfulness but scientists still don't know. Spectacular manoeuvres include the breach (where they jump almost completely out of the water and crash on their backs), the pectoral slap (where they lie on the water and slap one or both pectoral fins), and the tail slap (where they submerge almost vertically and slap their flukes on the surface). One of the more curious acts is the so-called spy hop, where the head pops vertically out of the water to eye level as if for a look-see before quietly slipping back down again.

Humpbacks produce the longest and most varied songs in the animal world – the only great whales to do so. Both males and females make sound but only the males 'sing', usually in the breeding season. Song sequences can last for 20 minutes. They're characteristic of particular populations and evolve over time. Scientists don't know why humpbacks do this – maybe the songs function as mating calls and/or warnings to other males, or to keep family groups together.

Humpbacks were hunted almost to extinction for their blubber and baleen. Whaling stations on Moreton Island, out to sea on Norfolk Island and further south at Byron Bay and Eden had reduced the east Australian humpback population from more than 10,000 down to maybe 300 before whaling finally stopped in 1962.

Recovery since then has been slow. A female calves every two to three years after an 11-12-month gestation, and then nurses her calf for a year on milk with a 35% fat content (human milk has 2%). The calf reaches maturity in 10 years.

The oldest humpbacks are about 50 years but they may get (much) older than that. Nobody really knows because of past whaling.

Dugongs

The shallow seagrass beds in Great Sandy Strait are one of Australia's most important feeding grounds for the dugong (*Dugong dugon*), our only marine mammal herbivore. The dugong and its North American counterpart, the manatee, form the order of *Sirenia* (sea cows), which are related to elephants. Instead of hind limbs, dugongs have a horizontally flattened tail, while the forelimbs are modified as paddles with which they strut along the seagrass.

These large, docile creatures can travel at 20km/hr but generally only cover distances of 25km a day. Calves ride on their mothers' backs. Dugongs may live for up to 50 years.

During 1992 Fraser Island experienced two cyclones which caused heavy siltation, leading to the demise of large areas of seagrass. Dugong numbers plummeted from an estimated 2000 to about 500. The seagrass beds are beginning to re-establish and dugong numbers are increasing, though it may take many years for the population to recover fully.

Fish

Freshwater Fish

The lakes and creeks support over 30 species of freshwater fish, though their numbers are limited and their ranges restricted by the isolation of the lakes. Lake Wabby is an exception, being home to nine species, including the rare **honey blue-eye** (*Pseudomugil mellis*), which has also been found in wallum creeks. More common in Fraser Island's waters are **rainbow fish** (*Melanotaenia duboulayi* and *Rhadinocentrus ornatus*). Carp gudgeon and a unique species of sunfish have also been found. The introduced **mosquito fish** (*Gambusia holbrooki*) competes with native fish for food, but fortunately it occurs only in a few Fraser Island streams.

It is believed that fish eggs first arrived in these isolated dune lakes on birds' feet.

Marine Fish

The island's estuaries and mangroves are important nurseries for young fish, while the coastal waters attract large numbers of fish that come here to feed and breed. In turn, they attract large numbers of fishing enthusiasts keen to hone their surf-fishing skills.

For more about Fraser Island's wide range of marine fish, see Fishing on p103. ■

Whale off Fraser Island

FRANK STOFFELS

Chapter Two

Planning The Trip

Information Sources

There is no shortage of information about the island, but where to begin? The following list of resources may help.

Tourist Offices

These information centres can help you find a tourist service or package to suit your needs:

Fraser Coast South Burnett Regional Tourism Board
Ph (07) 4191 2600, fax (07) 4191 2699
Toll-free ph 1800 444 155
www.frasercoastholidays.info
info@frasercoast.org.au

Hervey Bay Visitor Information Centre
227 Maryborough Rd, Hervey Bay
Ph (07) 4125 9855, fax (07) 4124 7626
toll-free ph 1800 811 728
www.visitherveybay.info
tourismhb@frasercoast.qld.gov.au

Maryborough and Fraser Island Visitor Information Centre
City Hall, Kent Street, Maryborough 4650
Ph (07) 4190 5742, fax (07) 4123 2533
Toll-free ph 1800 214 789
tourismmb@frasercoast.qld.gov.au
www.visitmaryborough.info

EPA Offices

Day-to-day management of the island is mainly carried out by the Environmental Protection Agency (EPA). Its offices can answer most questions about the island itself rather than its tourism business, and have lots of material on hand. The EPA website (www.epa.qld.gov.au) provides plenty of information, including a conditions report which is updated fortnightly. See Vehicle Permits later in this chapter for addresses and contact details of relevant EPA offices.

Eurong EPA Office

A EPA office is located on the island at:

Eurong (head office)   Ph (07) 4127 9128

The Eurong EPA office is open 8am-3.30pm Tuesday to Thursday, with variable hours Friday to Monday.

The EPA office issues camping permits if you wish to stay longer than your permit allows, and stock a range of brochures. The Eurong office even screens videos and sells books, posters and maps. The large display shelter next to the Central Station office is well worth a look.

The rangers sometimes provide guided tours and activities, especially during peak periods – check at the EPA office.

The island's police station (see page 44) is next to the Eurong EPA office.

FIDO

The Fraser Island Defenders Organization (FIDO) was founded in 1971 by the amateur naturalist, John Sinclair, to oppose sand-mining on the island. FIDO's ultimately successful campaign prompted *The Australian* newspaper to name Mr Sinclair Australian of the Year in 1976.

FIDO's focus also extended to logging and the organisation played a key role in Fraser Island's listing for World Heritage status. Today it keeps a watchful eye on environmental policies (dingo management, light-rail proposal) as well as the harmful (and beneficial) effects of tourism and real-estate developments.

FIDO's opinions can be a bit intense at times ("the Greenpeace of Fraser Island"), but its newsletter, *Moonbi* (the Butchulla name for the central part of the island), is a treasure-trove of information. Anyone with an ongoing interest in the island is well advised to read it – an archive is available on the website at www.fido.org.au.

For more information, or to become a member ($15), contact FIDO through the website or at PO Box 909, Toowong Q 4066.

FRANK STOFFELS

Planning The Trip

Useful Websites

If you type "Fraser Island" into the Google search engine you'll get 80,000 hits. Try some of the following sites instead, and use the links they provide:

www.environment.gov.au/heritage/places/world/fraser
– Department of the Environment and Heritage's Fraser Island page

http://dkd.net/fraser
– interesting online travel guide published by a Maryborough resident

www.frasercoastholidays.info – Fraser Coast South Burnett Regional Tourism Board, with more information and links than you can shake a computer mouse at

www.herveybay.qld.gov.au – Tourism Hervey Bay

www.sunzine.net/frasercoast – general tourism information

www.hervey.com.au – travel, reservations and community guide for the Hervey Bay region, with useful links to tour operators

www.boxatrix.com – general tourism information on the Fraser Coast, with lots of links

http://discover-fraserisland.netfirms.com – site hosted by a Hervey Bay internet and digital picture service provider, with lots of information, photos and links

www.fraserislandaccommodation.net
– lots of links to tour operators and some of the more upmarket accommodation options

www.fraserislandbackpackers.com – tours for the young at heart

www.fido.org.au – Fraser Island Defenders Organization (FIDO), which aims to ensure the wisest use of the island's resources (see previous page); great newsletter archive

http://friendsoffraserisland.org – campaigning to keep Fraser Island open for everyone to enjoy; critical of what it describes as "that small group of killjoys [read: FIDO] who would lock everyone out of Fraser Island unless they traveled on a conducted, controlled tour"

http://whc.unesco.org/en/list/630
– the UNESCO's World Heritage site (click on the Fraser Island link)

www.acfonline.org.au
– Australian Conservation Foundation site, then log on to the Fraser Island page

www.travelhops.com/Australia/Queensland/Fraser-Island
– lots of links to accommodation, tours, transport services, you name it

www.vnc.qld.edu.au/enviro/flinders/f-p-qfi.htm
– Fraser Island page on the site commem-orating Matthew Flinders' 1802 circumnavigation of Australia, with several interesting links down the bottom

www.epa.qld.gov.au/nature_ conservation/cyberrangers
– EPA's online nature club for kids

Sandy Cape   ROB BOEGHEIM

PHOTO: ROB BOEGHEIM

Books

We'd like to think that the book you're reading right now is the best general-purpose guide for the adventurous visitor. Several others can add to the experience though, including:

- Sinclair, John, 1997, *Discovering Fraser Island & Cooloola*, Australian Environmental Publications, Gladesville NSW – authoritative overview of the geology, ecosystems, history and natural life forms of the Great Sandy region, written by the founder of the Fraser Island Defenders Organization; includes detailed flora & fauna listings and extensive historical timeline
- Hincliffe, David and Julie, 2006, *Explore Fraser Island*, Great Sandy Publications, Robe SA - a good general overview of the island
- Burger, Angela, 2001, *Fraser Island* – written by a long-term resident and former co-owner of Eurong Beach Resort; provides an account of the major attractions, with revealing and often hilarious anecdotes from the past and present
- McCarthy, Brad, 2003, *Fraser Island: the essential visitors guide*, Dirty Weekends Australia Pty Ltd, Northgate Qld – ring-bound pocket guide with comprehensive accommodation listing (including photos and location maps) and detailed route directions
- Williams, Fred, 2002, *Princess K'Gari's Fraser Island* – fascinating account of the island's history, with many unique historical photos
- Miller, Olga, 1993, *Fraser Island Legends*, Jacaranda Press, Milton Qld – Butchulla legends retold by one of the prime elders
- Harmon-Price, Pamela, 1998, *Fraser Island: world heritage area: treasures in the sand*, Dept of Environment and Heritage, Brisbane – affordable coffee-table souvenir of the Fraser Island experience, with great photos

Maps

The maps in this book should suffice for general bushwalking purposes, as the trails are well defined and signposted and it's hard to get lost. EPA advises anyone intending to follow the Fraser Island Great Walk to carry the Fraser island Great Walk topographic map – available from the EPA Customer Service Centre. Hema's 1:130,000 *Fraser Island* map shows all the maps in this book on a single sheet so you get the complete overview. The reverse side has descriptions of the sights and extensive contact listings. Kingfisher Bay Resort sells the same map but with a different cover.

The QLD Department Natural Resources and Water (DNRW) 1:140,000 *Fraser Island* map is similar, but with relief shading instead of contour lines to show altitude. It too has descriptions of sights on the reverse. DNRW also puts out a series of 1:25,000 topographic image maps of the island based on aerial photos. They're beautifully produced and great to look at (you can just about make out individual trees!), but probably not as easy to navigate unless you're an experienced map reader.

The maps that come with your EPA *Fraser Island Information Pack* (see Vehicle Permits) are basic and not really intended for navigation.

Climate & When to Go
Seasons

Fraser Island's subtropical climate is pretty good year-round, with the ocean moderating the extremes of heat and cold.

That said, conditions can get pretty hot in **summer** (December-February) with daytime temperatures in the 30s, though the humidity levels are bearable. Biting insects such as March flies and mosquitoes are at their worst, and late summer brings the possibility of cyclones and rain.

Rainfall peaks in March, the beginning of **autumn** (March-May), with an average precipitation of 135-140mm, well above that on the mainland. The weather clears up quite rapidly towards the end of autumn, when daytime temperatures drop to a pleasant 30 degrees.

Winter (June-August) offers stable weather with daytime temperatures in the mid-20s, though water in the lakes may be too cold for swimming. That's because temperatures at night can drop to six degrees or even less in the inland forest areas, making warm sleeping bags advisable. But it's a good time to be active and go bushwalking.

Planning The Trip

Things warm up again in **spring** (September-November), though the weather remains stable and agreeable and this is probably the best time to visit. Wildflowers bloom from August to October, the tailor-fishing season is in full swing from July to October, and whales cavort in Hervey Bay on their annual migration to the southern ocean from August to the middle of October, peaking in early September.

The prevailing south-easterly winds can be quite strong at any time of year but tend to be gentler during the winter months. Be prepared for this when camping, especially along the eastern beach. Find a sheltered spot, use long 'sand pegs', and expect sand to get in everywhere.

Crowds

Book accommodation and (where possible) camping sites well in advance during public holidays and especially the Queensland school holidays, when the island gets packed to capacity. The busiest times are the two weeks around Christmas, the Easter period and the September (spring) school holidays. Accommodation prices in these peak periods are often higher as well. June (winter school holidays) also gets busy but tends to be a bit too cold for huge crowds. Weekends and especially long weekends attract day-trippers and overnighters.

Check the dates for Queensland school holidays at http://education.qld.gov.au.

Permits

All of Fraser Island (with the exception of a few freehold areas and townships) is protected as a national park under the Recreation Areas Management (RAM) Act, and is managed by the Environmental Protection Agency (EPA). Visitors require a permit if they wish to bring a vehicle onto the island, and a separate camping permit in order to camp anywhere except in the three private campgrounds.

Vehicle Permits

A Vehicle Service Permit (VSP) must be obtained before entering the area. This costs $33.45 for a month (or for the duration of the visit in the case of hire vehicles) or $167.45 for a year (Please note that VSP fees change each July). Refunds are available only in certain circumstances.

The VSP tag with the booking number should be fixed to the windscreen, and comes with an informative *Fraser Island Information Pack* that you're well advised to read before you head across. Among other things, it spells out the main rules and regulations on the island and can help avoid a hefty fine. The information is updated regularly, so read it even if you've visited before.

75-Mile Beach

ROB BOEGHEIM

Vehicle Service Permits can be ordered online at www.epa.qld.gov.au, through the Integrated Call Centre on 13 13 04 or at the following permit-issuing centres:

- EPA Customer Service,
  Ph (07) 3227 8185, nqic@epa.qld.gov.au,
  160 Ann St, **Brisbane**
  (8:30am-5pm Mon-Fri)

- EPA Rainbow Beach office,
  Ph (07) 5486 3160,
  Rainbow Beach Rd, **Rainbow Beach**
  on the southern outskirts of town
  (7am-4pm daily)

- EPA Maryborough office,
  Ph (07) 4121 1800, cnr Alice & Lennox Sts,
  Maryborough (9am-5pm Mon-Fri)

- EPA Bundaberg office,
  Ph (07) 4131 1600, 46 Quay Street,
  Bundaberg (8:30am-5pm Mon-Fri)

- EPA Great Sandy Info Centre,
  Ph (07) 5449 7792, 240 Moorindil Street,
  Tewantin (8am-4pm daily)

- River Heads Info Kiosk,
  Ph (07) 4125 8473,
  barge landing car park, **River Heads**
  (6:30am-3:30pm daily)

- Marina Kiosk,
  Ph (07) 4128 9800, Buccaneer Avenue,
  Urangan boat harbour (7am-6pm daily)

Camping Permits

A camping permit is required to camp anywhere on the island, except in the private campgrounds at Cathedral Beach and Kgari Camping Area (EPA camping permits don't cover these venues). This applies regardless of whether you're camping 'freelance' or in a designated campground with toilets and showers. The permit must be displayed clearly on the camping structure. Obtain it in advance online at www.epa.qld.gov.au, through the Integrated Call Centre on 13 13 04 or at the permit-issuing centres (see the previous section). Permits are also required to bush camp – bookings can be made online at www.epa.qld.gov.au or through the Integrated Call Centre on 13 13 04.

It costs $4.85 per person per night or $19.40 per family (up to two adults accompanying children aged under 18); children aged under 5 are free. The maximum length of stay is 22 days. Refunds are granted only in certain circumstances. Cutting your trip short for bad weather is not a valid request. (Please note that camping fees change each July.)

You nominate and pay for the number of nights when obtaining the permit. If you're not sure how long you're staying, or you intend to spend some nights at a resort but don't know how many or decide to extend your stay – you can also get your permit(s) from the EPA office at Eurong as you go along, but you must do so before you set up camp. Opening times vary and may be limited to a couple of hours a day, which can be rather inconvenient. It is always best to get your permits before going to the island. Fines apply if you camp without a permit.

A camping permit is required to camp anywhere on the island, except in the privately owned campgrounds

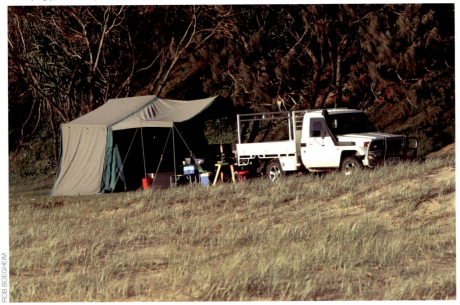

ROB BOEGHEIM

Environmental Concerns

The Butchulla people kindly request that you respect the land. You can do so by acting responsibly, and in the process help preserve this unique but fragile environment for future generations.

The Nature Conservation Act 1992 includes the following rules relevant to the island:

- No camping without a camping permit. The permit is only valid for the number of people and the time stated.
- No domestic animals can be taken into or kept in the area.
- All plants, animals and natural and cultural resources are protected and must not be disturbed or damaged.
- Don't feed any wildlife or leave any food, which may be scavenged.
- Take all rubbish with you, or place it in the bins provided. Don't bury it or leave it in fireplaces.
- Do not pollute watercourses with shampoos, soaps, detergents or other substances. Sunscreens and particularly insect repellents will cause pollution in lakes.
- Campfires are not permitted except in constructed fireplaces. Observe fire bans or restrictions and take extreme care with fire at all times.

- Don't collect firewood. Use only the firewood provided in designated campgrounds.
- Plants and plant material (other than food) must not be taken into the area without written authority.
- Appliances such as axes can only be used to split firewood or drive tent pegs. Machetes are not permitted.
- Vehicles must have current registration and third-party insurance and must only be driven by a licensed driver.
- Vehicles should only be driven on constructed roads, parking areas or routes and thoroughfares officially designated for vehicle use. Normal road rules apply.
- Minimise noise so as not to disturb other visitors, particularly between 9pm and 7am. Fraser Island campgrounds, as opposed to beach camping sites, have a 9pm noise curfew.
- Some beach camp sites allow generators up to 9pm, but these are signposted. Otherwise generators are not allowed.
- If camping in an area without toilet facilities, bury all human waste at least 50cm deep and at least 50m from lakes, watercourses, walking tracks, camping sites or public facilities.

See also Driving in the Getting Around chapter for rules and advice on minimising vehicle impact.

Sunset at Waddy Point

ROB BOEGHEIM

The **other side** of Fraser island

Mark Reed, a former forestry officer, used to work in remote parts of the island where he encountered some exotic hazards. Here, he provides a tongue-in-cheek account of experiences that visitors are highly unlikely to share unless they're careless or unfortunate, or both...

Back in the early 1980s, I was fortunate to spend part of my forestry officer training working on-site on Fraser Island. Since then, I have revisited the island many times and have covered virtually every track. It's a great place to visit and full of surprises.

The then Department of Forestry was in the process of closing down its logging activities. With the last log barges disappearing, attention focused on restoration and monitoring the recovery of the worst flogged (err, logged) sites. Much of this work took place in the 'restricted' northwestern quarter of the island. Here we experienced a different Fraser Island to the tame tranquillity of Central Station.

The territory demanded constant vigilance as it seemed that in addition to building Fraser out of sand, the Almighty Builder decided to pack every spring-loaded nasty of the insect, spider and reptile world into the very areas we had to access for these wretched research plots. I clearly remember thinking we simply didn't belong there.

This area of the island is rich with critters doing as they do without human intervention. You can be walking through the bush and get treated to a display so ridiculous that it would be laughed out of the cinema if it hit the big screen. One day I was carrying an armful of survey pegs and felt myself pulled up by a spider web that would make Spiderman's threads seem like overcooked vermicelli.

Tinted yellow, the web was bizarre in its strength and adhesive properties. Equally bizarre was the bird-eating spider of gargantuan proportions doing push-ups in the corner. To avoid panic and excess adrenalin of the wrong kind, it pays to wave a stick in front of you when walking through the bush.

Shaken and flushed by the manic dance of shoulder-slapping one does after such an encounter, the march progressed less than 100m before coming upon another Fraser Island phenomenon – the stumpy dullness of the death adder. These snakes are lazy creatures whose hunting regime exists of lying dead still so as to impersonate a stick, waiting for dinner to blunder along. Step on one of these snakes and you are in serious trouble as they are extremely poisonous. So don't rush along looking at the treetops in the Fraser Island bush.

The beach was always a welcome sight at the end of a day with such spooky creatures, even if they were fascinating in their weirdness. However, the surprises could continue there too.

Just north of Waddy Point is a sheltered stretch of water that is popular with the fishing fraternity, who launch their boats and then clean them before winding them back onto their trailers for the long haul down the beach.

Cleaning all the burley and fish parts off the boats into the water has a magnetic effect on the local sharks. On one memorable occasion, I watched a large shark shoot up from the dark water to swim sideways at high speed through the water immediately behind two boats that were nosed onto the beach. The water couldn't have been more than 60cm deep and this three-metre monster shot through, snapping its mouth open and shut on the scrap-stained water. About 50m up the beach, a mother was happily watching her kids playing in the waist-deep shallows. In case you are wondering, yes, I did point out the danger.

Another tip concerns driving on the beach, particularly if you are heading south on the eastern beach late in the day. Shadows can come in many mysterious shapes and forms. Some can be real, some can be damp patches of sand or, as we discovered one night to our great horror, some can be rocks!

If you must drive on the beach late in the day or early in the evening, do so with extreme care and if you are unsure about what is ahead, stop and look. There are only a few rock patches on the beach, but take note of exactly where they are and keep track of your mileage so you know when they are getting near.

There are a thousand tales that could have the budding Fraser traveller paranoid beyond reason, so we won't talk about the surprising prevalence of trap-door spiders and things like that. Take careful note of the driving tips section in this book, pack your sense of humour and find out about the magic place for yourself. It's worth the effort!

Special Precautions

Fraser Island is a great place for a holiday and is generally quite safe. If you stick to the major tracks and sights, there will always be other people to lend a hand if something goes wrong. Facilities on the island are limited however (see below), so it pays to be self-sufficient.

The biggest risks consist of vehicle accidents and, unfortunately, dingoes. In both cases, trouble can be avoided by using common sense and following the advice in your Fraser Island Information Pack brochures. Read these carefully. Also see the sections in this book on Driving (pp55-63) and Dingoes (pp27-29).

The island has venomous snakes and spiders but you have to be very unlucky to encounter them, though the risk increases if you go bush-walking off the beaten track. However, we can almost guarantee that you will encounter sand flies, March flies and mosquitoes on the west coast and occasionally elsewhere, especially in the summer months. The relevant sections in this book offer advice on how to avoid them.

Be prepared for the fierce sun at any time of year, not just at the height of summer. Its effects are magnified by water and sand and its rays can burn you to a crisp even through cloud. Bring a wide-brimmed hat and sunglasses, cover up with a long-sleeved shirt and trousers, and use sunscreen if you're so inclined (but not when swimming in the lakes, where sunscreen lotions pose an environmental hazard).

Driving on the western beach is hazardous. Deep weed banks can be covered with a shallow layer of sand, appearing to offer a safe driving surface. Your vehicle will sink in these areas. Recovery could take a long time, meaning your vehicle may be swamped if the tide comes in.

Unfortunately there have been cases of theft from vehicles and camping sites left unattended. Take the necessary precautions, including travel insurance.

Police

In all emergencies, dial 000 (or 112 from a mobile). The island's police station is at Eurong, Ph (07) 4127 9288. If you get no reply, try the police stations on the mainland at Hervey Bay, Ph (07) 4128 5333, or Tin Can Bay, Ph (07) 5486 2426.

Medical Emergencies

There's no hospital or health clinic, but an ambulance operates out of Happy Valley during the Queensland and NSW school holidays, Ph (07) 4127 9158. At other times, and for emergencies requiring helicopter evacuation, ring the general emergency number, 000, or if on a mobile, dial112. Alternatively, contact the police station at Eurong (see the previous section).

Carry a first-aid kit, including insect repellent and anti-itching lotion against sand flies on the west coast. Also bring all your medications.

Report any dingo close encounters, nips, stalkings or attacks to the nearest ranger or ranger station. Try to note identifying features of the animal.

Communication
Telephone

Mobile phone reception is reasonable to good on the west side of the island and in the south, where you can pick up signals from the mainland. On the east side, the centre and the north, however, you'd be very lucky to get a connection. Satellite phones (satphones) work fine everywhere, of course, but they're still rather expensive.

There are public phones at Kingfisher Bay, Eurong, Happy Valley, Cathedral Beach and Orchid Beach, at the ranger stations (Eurong, Central Station, Dundubara and Waddy Point), as well as at Yidney Rocks Cabins and Indian Head. Bring plenty of coins.

Post & Internet

There's no post office on the island, but stamps and postpaks are available at Kingfisher Bay, Eurong, Happy Valley, Cathedral Beach and Orchid Beach. You'll find letterboxes there too.

Kingfisher Bay, Eurong and Happy Valley have coin-operated internet booths, though the connections can be a bit unreliable and you may have to be patient.

Radio

Some people bring a CB radio to talk with other vehicles in their convoy; others will be equipped with HF radio to talk with the world at large. If you don't have either, it's probably not worth bothering with the investment just for Fraser Island.

Oddly enough, you can receive ABC Classic FM clear as a piccolo all over the island. If this means a lot to you, you're in luck!

Shopping

The townships all have general stores, open daily from 8am to somewhere between 5pm and 6.30pm, but choice is limited and prices can be high. The best plan is to try for self-sufficiency. Bring all the gear and supplies you're likely to need – especially spare parts that suit your vehicle – and then rely on the island facilities for the basic supplies, such as bread, milk and ice. Do use the shops on the island as continued patronage ensures their survival.

There are bakeries at Eurong and Kingfisher Bay, with fresh bread, pies and cakes – a treat if you've been roughing it for several days. Many shops get fresh bread daily from Hervey Bay.

Bring plenty of batteries for torches etc – they cost a lot here – and any slide film you think you'll need (print film is readily available) along with spare memory for the video or digital camera. Most of the shops have EFTPOS but it doesn't harm to bring enough cash as well.

Dining

You can have sit-down meals at Kingfisher Bay, Eurong and Happy Valley. Kingfisher has several restaurants, including the very pleasant, alfresco Sand Bar pub and bistro/pizzeria near the jetty, which also has a saltwater pool to keep the kids amused.

The alfresco Satinay Bar & Bistro at Happy Valley's Fraser Island Wilderness Retreat, built from local hardwoods, is just as relaxing. The dining at Eurong is good as well, though the restaurant in the central resort building which overlooks the swimming pool can get busy with bus tour groups at lunchtime.

Takeaway food is available at the above resorts, as well as Cathedral Beach and Orchid Beach, though choice may be limited to the token pies and sausage rolls. The bakeries at Kingfisher and Eurong are good places for a tasty snack. ■

The Sand Bar near the Kingfisher Bay jetty

Chapter Three

Where To Stay

Camping on the island is very popular because it's such a great way to experience the unique natural environment. Nothing beats waking up to the dawn chorus of the birds and enjoying a first cup of tea in the early-morning sun.

Not everyone enjoys this 'million-star' accommodation however, and even campers may wish to treat themselves to the occasional luxury of a proper bed under a roof. Fortunately the island has a wide range of options, from lavish resorts where everything is laid on, to motel-style rooms, self-catering homes and villa units, basic cabins and dormitory-style bunk rooms.

The main resorts are Kingfisher Bay, Eurong, Happy Valley and Cathedral Beach, which offer many types of accommodation including self-contained holiday houses and cabins. Other (self-contained) accommodation can be found at Happy Valley, Yidney Rocks/The Oaks, Second Valley, Orchid Beach, Indian Head and Poyungan Rocks. See pages 50-53 for further information.

Camping

There's a choice of several EPA-serviced and EPA-established campgrounds (the latter with fewer if any facilities), three privately managed campgrounds, beach camping zones or hiker's camps. There is no camping at Kingfisher Bay or Eurong.

Camping anywhere on the island – except at the three privately managed grounds – requires a EPA camping permit (see p41).

Beach camping zones are usually unsheltered from ocean winds, have no facilities and overall are less comfortable than the serviced or established campgrounds. No-camping zones are clearly signed along the beach, and fines apply for camping there. Roughing it may be one of the charms of camping, but irresponsible beach camping can also ruin vital coastal dunes. To protect the beauty of the island, opt for a serviced or established campground first. Families with children should select fenced campgrounds (Central Station, Dilli Village, Lake Boomanjin, Dundubara and Waddy Point).

Beware of dingoes – lock all food in the vehicle or use dingo-proof lockers where provided. Dingoes will rip tents open in search of food.

Smelly shoes, women's used hygiene products, wine casks, beer spills and oils may also attract them. Hikers should consider putting anything that may attract them in their pack and hoisting it up a tree if there are no dingo-proof lockers.

Where bush toileting is necessary, dig a 50cm deep hole and cover your toilet paper and waste. Again, be dingo-aware. You are very vulnerable in this position, so never go alone and always cover your waste. Dingoes will be attracted to this.

Open campfires are no longer permitted, the Fraser-friendly alternative is to choose fuel stoves. Propane (camping gas) is available at Kingfisher Bay, Eurong, Happy Valley, Cathedral Beach and Orchid Beach. Campfires are only allowed in the communal fire rings at Dundubara and Waddy Point campgrounds.

EPA Campgrounds

The EPA manages campgrounds with facilities (showers, picnic tables, barbecues, toilets and tap water) at Central Station, Lake Boomanjin, Wathumba, Waddy Point and Dundubara. Central Station's great campground is nestled amid the rainforest. The campgrounds at Central Station, Waddy Point and Dundubara have hot showers (bring plenty of 50c and $1 coins). The site at Lake McKenzie is now day-use only to allow it to regenerate, but there's a hikers-only campground.

Bookings are required for Central Station, Dundubara and Waddy Point (top and beach-front) campgrounds, as well as the One Tree Rocks beach camping zone. You're strongly advised to book several months in advance for school-holiday periods – online at www.epa .qld.gov.au/parks or csc@epa.qld.gov.au; or by ringing 13 13 04 or fax 1300 300 768; or by visiting one of the EPA customer service centres (see p37).

Other EPA campgrounds are 'established' rather than serviced, which means limited facilities and little supervision. The one at Ungowa has toilets and a dingo safe, and Garrys Anchorage has a picnic table and rainwater tank, but that's about as far as it goes. Bring all rubbish out from these areas.

Left: Palms provide a pleasant ambience at Eurong Beach Resort

Private Campgrounds

There are three privately managed campgrounds on the island. **Frasers at Cathedral Beach** (Map p121, D7) has spacious camping sites in pleasant surroundings, with hot showers, toilets, drinking water and a laundry.

The resort also has two "Canvas under Canvas" sites consisting of ready-made tents on timber floors with screen door, window, pillows, blankets and sheets supplied, along with a fully self-contained kitchen. These are only available by booking through Fraser Island Company Tours (ph 1800 063 933).

The **Dilli Village campground** (Map p124, B4) welcomes partying backpacker groups and doesn't have the usual 9pm noise curfew, and is well fenced against dingoes. Forget about the former sand-miners' cottages here, though: they've become a bit decrepit and are no longer rented out.

About 4km south, just inland from the Pinnacles, is the Butchulla-run **Kgari Camping**

Safari tent, Kgari Camping Area

Area (Map p121, E6). It used to be known as Thoorgine, but that fell into disrepair until it was taken over by new managers under a new name. They wasted no time clearing lantana and installing several facilities, and have turned it into a pleasant place to linger a while and pick up on some Aboriginal culture.

Camping at Wathumba

Facilities are a bit more basic than at Cathedral Beach and include solar-powered hot showers, three screened rotundas with raised floorboards and cooking facilities, a "safari tent" (a ready-made tent on a raised timber deck) and the usual camping bays. The rotundas are ideal for groups, who can simply roll out their swags and don't need to bother with tents. Aboriginal tours and shows are in planning, but meanwhile the supervisor, Joe, is happy to explain the island's Aboriginal heritage and may even play his didgeridoo.

The owners kindly request that you respect their no-alcohol policy.

'Freelance' Camping

Beach camping is allowed at undeveloped 'beach' camping zones along the both coasts (usually located between the foredunes and larger secondary dunes – see the maps) and some spots on the west coast. Signs will tell you where camping is not allowed.

Beach camping zones, with no facilities, have been set up along both coasts (see the maps for details).

There are also the EPA-established sites in the south-west at Coolooloi Creek, Snout Point, Fig Tree Point, Garrys Anchorage and Ungowa.

When beach camping, find shelter from the south-easterly winds, use long 'sand pegs' and expect sand to get in everywhere. Do not set up within 50m of any creek, or as directed by signs. In the interior, do not camp within 100m of any lake. Always stick to camping sites that have already been used by others (don't create new ones), use fuel stoves (open fires are not permitted), and remove all rubbish. Bury toilet waste at least 50cm deep.

Beach access at Happy Valley

The campground at Central Station

The ablutions block at Central Station

Resorts

Kingfisher Bay Resort

(Map p122, C3)
Ph 1800 072 555, (07) 4120 3333
www.kingfisherbay.com
reservations@kingfisherbay.com

Main pool at the Kingfisher Bay Resort

This resort, at North White Cliffs on the western side of the island, was at the cutting edge of environmental management and design when it opened in 1992. Buildings are below the tree line and are limited to two levels and where possible designed around major trees. The colours – greens, burgundy and golden browns – are those of its bush surroundings, and the Queensland-style wooden buildings with open verandas have curving tin roofs reflecting the rolling sand dunes. The old sand-mining barge off the ferry jetty acts as a breakwater.

Facilities include four swimming pools (the main one in the shape of Lake McKenzie), a spa, tennis courts, fishing clinic, 4WD hire, three restaurants, four bars, conference facilities, a bakery and coffee shop, and a beauty and massage salon. Day visitors can relax at the beachfront pavilion (near the ferry landing) with bar, bistro and pool. Petrol, diesel, ice, groceries, camping supplies, resort wear and souvenirs are available from the shopping village.

The resort has its own staff of rangers – 22 of them, the largest privately operated ranger team in Australia – who conduct free daily nature walks and activities as well as 4WD tours and marine cruises. Kids enjoy the free Junior Eco Ranger programme on weekends and school holidays, and a Kids Club is open all year for those aged under five. Whale watch tours are available from August to October.

You can book a luxurious room in this world-class resort hotel, or self-contained accommodation including:

- two-bedroom villas
- three-bedroom villas
- A number of B&B packages including catamaran transfers and tours, and all-in packages such as the popular Wilderness Adventure Tour for 18 to 35-year-olds

Check the website for further details. The resort also has fully furnished two- and three-bedroom villas and blocks of freehold land for sale. Again, check the website.

Eurong Beach Resort

(Map p123, F5)
Ph 1800 111 808, (07) 4127 9122
www.fraser-is.com
enquiries@eurong.com

This resort sits amid acres of appealing lawns and gardens on the edge of the ocean beach, 32km from Fraser's southern tip. A complex containing a restaurant, lounges, bars, and conference and function rooms overlooks a large, free-form swimming pool.

There are two bars open to the public, with takeaway liquor sales. The general store has groceries, fuel supplies, camping gear, fishing tackle and ice, and the bakery (one of only two on the island) sells delicious fresh breads, cakes and snacks. Four-wheel-drive coach tours operate daily to/from Eurong, Hervey Bay, the Sunshine Coast and Rainbow Beach. There are tennis courts, 4WD hire vehicles, charter joy flights and the resort's own bitumen airstrip. EFTPOS facilities are available.

Accommodation options, all with private facilities and fully equipped kitchens or kitchenettes, include the following:

- luxury apartments with private veranda and two bedrooms sleeping up to six people.
- motel units with private veranda or patio, and double or twin beds with a lounge to make two more single beds for children.
- A-frame cottages for up to five people
- cabins for safari or education groups, with four bunks and exclusive use of an amenities block, a camp kitchen and a roofed alfresco dining area
- a number of all-in packages that include tours, accommodation, meals and transfers

Check the website for further details.

Where To Stay

Fraser Island Backpackers YHA Happy Valley

(Map p123, B7)
Ph (07) 4127 9144
www.fraserislandco.com.au
backpackers@fraserislandco.com.au

This attractively situated, peaceful resort is tucked into a hillside halfway along Fraser's east coast. It offers nine appealingly designed, self-contained lodges built from local timbers.

Guests can cater for themselves or enjoy the relaxed atmosphere of the Satinay Bar and Bistro, which is open for breakfast, lunch and dinner and also provides snacks and takeaway meals throughout the day. A swimming pool and barbecue area complete this quiet setting.

A convenience store provides souvenirs, liquor supplies and a range of everyday needs including petrol, diesel, drinking water and ice. EFTPOS facilities are available.

Frasers at Cathedral Beach

(Map p121, D7)
Ph (07) 3512 8100
www.cathedralbeach.com.au
info@travelonline.com

The most modest of the four resorts (there's no restaurant, for instance) hides in the coastal bush-land behind the beach that takes its name from the stunning line of coloured sand cliffs called The Cathedrals. Formerly known as Cathedral Beach Resort, it's a pleasant, casual sort of place surrounded by native trees and cool palms without other residential developments in the area. The beach fishing here is particularly good.

Apart from the camping options discussed earlier, the resort offers self-contained cabins in two- or three-bedroom configurations.

There's a mini supermarket which sells snacks, fresh meat and fish, general supplies, souvenirs and ice; a bottle shop; and a petrol, diesel, and camping gas outlet. EFTPOS facilities are available.

Access to Happy Valley

The relaxing Satinay Bar & Bistro

Fraser Island Backpackers, Happy Valley

Holiday Houses & Other Options

There are many forms of self-contained accommodation other than those offered by the resorts described above. Sometimes they're cheaper but often they're not, though they may provide a bit more seclusion and privacy. They range from basic holiday shacks that sleep two, all the way up to large, luxurious houses that sleep 10 or more.

Prices start at about $100 a night and go (way) up from there, depending on the number of people (including babies and children) and time of year. Prices are often higher during the peak periods of Christmas, Easter and the September school holidays, but not always. Bookings can be made for one night, two nights or per week (usually six nights and seven days), though many places require minimum stays of two nights or more. Discounts may apply to longer rental periods.

In short, it's impossible for us to provide price comparisons here. Check the websites, many of which have photos of the properties on offer. Better still, ring around – the proprietors may be willing to discuss special rates if business is slow. Walk-in rates may be lower as well, if you're lucky enough to find a place.

This type of accommodation usually includes a fully equipped kitchen and a TV, but check whether the price you're quoted includes sheets and pillows – you may have to pay more or bring your own.

Eurong (Map p123, F6)

Most of Eurong itself is taken up by Eurong Beach Resort's many accommodation structures. Other options include:

- **Fraser Island Property Sales Management and Accommodation** (Easton Street, Ray's Place, Talinga, Weeroona, Winduna) – Ph (07) 4127 9188, 0429 379 188, www.fraserservice.com.au, admin@fraserservice.com.au
- **Sanantonio's** Ph (07) 3289 2109, tony.san@bigpond.com

Eurong Second Valley
(Map p123, F5)

This quiet area immediately south of the Eurong resort has holiday houses favoured by family groups.

- **Cedar Lodge** Ph (02) 6297 0618, 0419 725 341
- **Fraser Island Beach Houses** Ph (07) 4127 9205, www.fraserislandbeachhouses.com.au, holiday@fraserislandbeachhouses.com.au
- **Fraser Island Property Sales Management and Accommodation** (Bow-Allum Place, BringABeerAlong, Castaway's on Fraser, Honeyeater Lodge, My Island Home, Nick's A Frame, Number 19, Reid's Place, Ryan's Bungalow, Seashell Lodge, Taxi House) – Ph (07) 4127 9188, 0429 379 188, www.fraserservice.com.au, admin@fraserservice. com.au
- **Isle Escape** Ph (07) 5597 0690, 0419 733 159, www.accommodationfraserisland.net
- **O'Dwyer's** Ph (07) 3341 7771
- **The Beach Cottage** Ph (07) 4127 9231, www.fraserislandhideaway. com, info@fraserislandhideaway. com
- **The Bungalow** Ph 0427 132 056, www.fraserislandbungalow.com.au, hbphty@bigpond.com
- **Windmill Cottage** Ph (07) 4127 9173, three-bedroom house (no microwave or TV).

Fishing at dawn along 75 Mile Beach

ROB BOEGHEIM

Fishing at Indian Head

Happy Valley & Surroundings
(Map p123, B7)

Happy Valley is appropriately named. The settlement is small and cosy and the surroundings are attractive. South along the beach, Yidney Rocks/The Oaks and Poyungan Rocks are good fishing spots with some appealing beachfront units.

- **Fraser Island Hideaway**
  Ph (07) 4127 9231,
  www.fraserislandhideaway.com,
  info@fraserislandhideaway.com:
  beautifully situated at Poyungan Valley,
  6km south of Happy Valley
- **Kurrawa**
  Ph (07) 4127 9113,
  www.kurrawa.flyingsaucepan.com
- **Poyungan Rocks** Ph (07) 4127 9440,
  www.fraserbeachfront.com.au
- **Yidney Rocks Beachfront Apartments**
  Ph (07) 4127 9113,
  www.yidneyrocks.com.au,
  maijan@yidneyrocks.com.au

Orchid Beach & Indian Head
(Map p119, D5)

Many tourists turn around after they've travelled north to Indian Head and the Champagne Pools, so Orchid Beach lacks the hustle and bustle of the other townships – which makes it an attractive getaway destination. It's also one of the few places on the island with ongoing residential developments, and there are plenty of holiday houses for rent. These include:

- **Marloo** Ph (07) 3359 1139,
- **Caretaker** (Brahminy, Calshaws, Gardner's, Langleys, Orchid Beach House, Sainsbury's, Vinclip, Waldie's) –
  Ph (07) 4127 9129
- **Langleys** Ph (07) 5445 2458,
  www.houseonfraser.com
- **Eliza Palms** Ph (07) 4127 9180,
  www.elizapalms.com
- **Orchid Beach Rental** (Bennett's Cottage, Bracefell House, Break See House, Crawford's Place, Eliza One, Karalee Sands, Marloo Chalet, Peter Loose's, Paper Bark, Scott's Place, Tree Tops) –
  Ph (07) 4127 9220,
- **Orchid Beach Property Rentals & Maintenance** (Boat Shed, Boughton's Bunkhouse, Driftwood, Duncampin, Eliza Doolittle, Grand View, La Sabbia, Marloo Blue, Munros' Oasis, Orchid Sands, The Sands, To Windward) – Ph (07) 4127 9266,
  www.fraserislandrentals.com,
  info@fraserislandrentals.com
- **Eliza One** Ph (07) 5494 3340,
  (07) 4127 9220 www.elizaone.com.au
- **Orchid House** Ph 0417 709 006,
  www.orchidhouse.com.au,
  info@orchidhouse.com.au
- **K'Gari** Ph 0411 519 614,
  www.kgari.com, simon@kgari.com

At Indian Head, a top fishing spot during the tailor season, check **Fraser Island Fishing Units**, Ph (07) 5449 9346, 0428 712 283. ■

ROB BOEGHEIM

Chapter Four

Getting Around

Getting to the Island

The main departure points to Fraser Island are Inskip Point (Rainbow Beach), Urangan Boat Harbour (Hervey Bay) and (Mary) River Heads.

From the south, drive north to Rainbow Beach via Gympie or Noosa and Tewantin. Either drive the conventional sealed road which links Gympie and Rainbow Beach, or take the 4WD route from Noosa/Tewantin along Cooloola's Teewah Beach at low tide past the impressive coloured sand cliffs up to Rainbow Beach (phone the rangers at Rainbow Beach to check if Mudlo Rocks are passable). From Rainbow Beach, head north to Inskip Point by travelling the sealed inland road all the way up, or by turning off part of the way up and driving along the Inskip Peninsula beach.

From the north, drive south along the Bruce Highway, turn towards the coast at Torbanlea and continue on through Hervey Bay to Urangan Boat Harbour or River Heads.

Bus companies travel to Rainbow Beach, Maryborough and Hervey Bay. Various privately operated passenger and vehicle barges and a water taxi travel between several locations on the island and the mainland (see Barges, below).

Queensland Rail has regular services from the north and south into Maryborough. Sunshine Express operates regional services to Maryborough and Hervey Bay three times a day, while charter flights are available from Brisbane, Hervey Bay, Rainbow Beach, Maryborough and the Sunshine Coast (see Flying, p65).

Private yachts and motor-sailers often anchor at Kingfisher Bay Resort, Wathumba and Garrys Anchorage (see Boating pp104-105). If you camp on the beach at Wathumba or Garrys Anchorage, you'll need a EPA camping permit. There is no camping at Kingfisher Bay Resort.

Driving (4WD)

Most people who visit the island independently do so by 4WD (two-wheel-drives are not permitted). There is no other way of getting around easily – at least not until the Fraser Island Defenders Organization realises its dream of a light rail system.

Some 20,000 vehicles visit the island every year and, in the hands of thoughtless drivers, 4WDs can have quite a negative effect on the environment (see "Minimising Vehicle Impact").

All the normal road rules apply, including blood-alcohol limits and seat belts – and yes, police on the island do check. The maximum speed on inland roads is 35km/h (but often it's best to stay well below that); on the eastern beach, 80km/h; in built-up areas and camping grounds, 20km/h. Keep to the left of oncoming vehicles.

For itineraries, see Driving pp 97-101.

What Type of 4WD?

A 'proper' 4WD with good ground clearance is essential if you want to enjoy driving here – see Rentals & Tours if you don't have your own. The inland tracks have deep ruts due to frequent traffic, and the soft, bottomless approach tracks to the beach often seem daunting. Dedicated 4WDs can take them in their stride if driven competently – vehicles such as LandCruisers, HiLuxes, Patrols, Pajeros, Jackaroos, Land/Range Rovers, Explorers, Grand Cherokees and the like.

The more car-like 4WDs, including so-called all-wheel-drives and 'crossover' vehicles, will tackle a lot of the island, but their low ground clearance is a limiting factor and they can get stuck easily. If you must drive one of these, keep tyre pressures as low as possible, try straddling the worst ruts rather than driving in them, and maintain engine revs and momentum. Take special care at the ferry landings and beach access tracks. Good luck!

The soft approach tracks to the beach often seem daunting

Left: Driving along Seventy-Five Mile Beach
PHOTO: TOURISM QUEENSLAND

ROB BOEGHEIM

Barges

The ferries connecting the island to the mainland are flat-bottomed barges that run up onto the beach. Make sure you've engaged 4WD and lowered your tyre pressures before you (dis)embark as the sand in these areas is well and truly churned up (see Driving, below).

The Inskip Point barges (*Manta-Ray* and *Rainbow Venture*) sail back and forth all day on the 15-minute crossing. *Rainbow Venture* doesn't require bookings, though if business is quiet you might want to call them over by phone.

The following prices and times may change at any time:

RAINBOW VENTURE *No bookings required*
Ph 1800 227 437,
www.kingfisherbay.com

Departure times from mainland and island
Inskip Point to Hook Point and vice versa
Between 7am and 5pm daily
Extended hours during school holidays, long weekends, Easter and on demand

Return fares (cash, credit card or cheque by prior arrangement)

Vehicle (including driver and three passengers)	$90
with trailer up to 6ft	$150
with trailer 7ft to18ft	$150
Additional passenger	$5
Motorcycle, including rider	$42.50

Single fare (cash, credit card or cheque by prior arrangement)

Vehicle	$65
with trailer up to 6ft	$100

Barges at Inskip Point

ROB BOEGHEIM

MANTA-RAY *Bookings preferred*
Ph (07) 5486 8888 or 0418 872 599,
www.fraserislandbarge.com.au,
manta-ray@rainbow-beach.org

Departure times from mainland
Inskip Point to Hook Point
from 6.30am on demand, with extended hours on demand

Departure times from island
Hook Point to Inskip Point
6.30am then on demand until 5.30pm (winter) or 6pm (summer)

Return fares (cash or credit card)

Vehicle, including driver	$90
with trailer	$150
Additional passenger	no charge
Motorcycle, including rider	$40

Single fares (cash or credit card)

Vehicle, including driver	$65
with trailer	$95

FRASER DAWN *Bookings required*
Ph 1800 227 437,
www.kingfisherbay.com

Departure times from mainland
Great Sandy Strait Marina, Urangan to Moon Point
Winter Season (1 April to 31 August):
8.30am, 3.30pm daily
Summer Season (1 September to 31 March):
8.30am, 4pm daily

Departure times from island
Moon Point to Great Sandy Straits Marina, Urangan
Winter Season (1 April to 31 August):
9.30am, 4.30pm daily
Summer Season (1 September to 31 March):
9.30am, 5pm daily

Return fares (cash only)

Vehicle (including driver and three passengers)	$150
with trailer up to 6ft	$210
with trailer 7ft to18ft	$250
Additional passenger	$11
Motorcycle, including one rider	$54
Walk-on passenger	$26

Single fares (cash only)

Vehicle (including driver and three passengers)	$85
with trailer up to 6ft	$125
with trailer 7ft to18ft	$145
Additional passenger	$6

Getting Around

FRASER VENTURE *Bookings required*

Ph 1800 227 437, www.kingfisherbay.com

Departure times from mainland
River Heads to Wanggoolba Creek
8.30am, 10.15am, 3.30pm daily

Departure times from island
Wanggoolba Creek to River Heads
9am, 2.30pm, 4pm daily

Return fares (cash only)

Vehicle (including driver and three passengers)	$150
with trailer up to 6ft	$210
with trailer 7ft to18ft	$250
Additional passenger	$11
Motorcycle with one rider	$54
Walk-on passenger	$26

Single fares (cash only)

Vehicle (including driver and three passengers)	$85
with trailer up to 6ft	$125
with trailer 7ft to18ft	$145
Additional passenger	$6

KINGFISHER BAY BARGES

Bookings required
Ph 1800 227 437,
www.kingfisherbay.com

Departure times from mainland
River Heads to Kingfisher Bay
7.15am, 12.30pm, 3pm daily

Departure times from island
Kingfisher Bay to River Heads
8.30am, 2pm, 4pm daily

Return fares (cash or credit card)

Vehicle (including driver and three passengers)	$150
with trailer up to 6ft	$210
with trailer 7ft to18ft	$250
Additional passenger	$11
Motorcycle, including one rider	$54

KINGFISHER BAY FAST CAT

Pre-book, passenger service only
Ph 1800 227 437,
www.kingfisherbay.com

Departure times from mainland
Urangan Boat Harbour to Kingfisher Bay
6.45am, 8.45am, 12pm, 4pm, 7pm, 10pm daily

Departure times from island
Kingfisher Bay to Urangan Boat Harbour
7.40am, 10.30am, 2pm, 5pm, 8pm, 11.30pm daily

Return fares (cash, EFTPOS or credit card)

Adult passenger	$55
Child passenger	$28

Trailers

Forget about caravans, but some fishers like to drag a boat along. This is not a very good idea in sand, especially in deep, soft sections such as the Indian Head bypass track that many fishers will want to negotiate in order to get to Waddy Point. Only attempt this if you have a suitable trailer and plenty of experience in sand.

Luggage trailers or (lightweight) camper trailers are smaller and less problematic, but they can still get you stuck and will make backing up very difficult when you encounter oncoming vehicles. At times they are simply not worth the trouble. Try your hardest to fit all the gear inside your vehicle and if necessary use a roof rack before considering a trailer.

Trailers should be designed for off-road use – i.e. solidly constructed with heavy-duty chassis, axles, springs, hangers and tow couplings – and should have enough ground clearance to handle the deeply rutted tracks.

Vehicle Preparation

Sand driving puts a lot of stress on a vehicle, so make sure it is in good condition. If a service is due, have this done before you set off, even if the service is a bit early. Repair facilities on the island are very limited (see Repairs & Towing).

Sand and salt are major enemies. They can work their way into any exposed moving part, so pump up all grease nipples. A good rust-proofing job is a wise investment as well, as salty moisture causes almost instantaneous corrosion. People in hire vehicles may enjoy driving through the water's edge on the eastern beach but private owners tend to avoid it like the plague and so they should – according to the tow-truck operators, the most common cause of breakdowns is salty moisture getting into the electronic components of modern vehicles.

Kingfisher barge

FRANK STOFFELS

Minimising vehicle impact

- As a general rule, **keep your vehicle in 4WD** on the island. It provides more control in the soft stuff (less involuntary swerving) and doesn't damage the tracks as much. However, see the section on Transmission Wind-Up.
- Lower your **tyre pressures** before arrival (see Tyres & Pressures p61)
- On the eastern beach, **stay on the hard surface between the low and high tide marks**. Around high tide, wait an hour or so instead of pushing through soft sand and/or damaging fragile vegetation.
- **Stay on the tracks** and don't go bush-bashing. When camping on the eastern beach, use tracks into the dunes that already exist – don't create new ones.
- **Be mindful of birds** on the eastern beach. Drive around them and keep your distance. Far too many have been killed by thoughtless drivers.
- When encountering oncoming vehicles on the inland tracks, **only use existing passing bays** and don't drive into the roadside vegetation – reverse to a previous passing bay if necessary.
- **Take care when manoeuvring at camping sites**, especially if the view is obscured by luggage in the vehicle and you're not entirely familiar with its dimensions.
- **Keep noise to a minimum.** Ensure the exhaust system is in good working order and don't rev the engine unnecessarily.

Getting Around

BRONWYN HEALING

Ngkala Rocks, one of the few parts of the island where low-ratio may be useful

ROB BOEGHEIM

Beware of sticks and other objects on the inland tracks that can 'stake' a tyre

Avoid driving through the water's edge – salty moisture in the electronic components is the most common cause of vehicle breakdown.

ROB BOEGHEIM

It's also important to clean the vehicle as soon as possible after your visit, in order to remove all sand and salt from the exterior, interior and engine bay. The underbody area in particular will need close attention. Seek out an underbody car wash on the mainland as you get off the ferry – it's money very well spent.

Back home, follow this up with a thorough hand wash top to bottom, front to back and inside out. Pump up the grease nipples again to expel any sand and salt that may have worked its way into the steering linkages, suspension components and what have you.

Spares & Tools

It's easy to go overboard on spares, but carry at least a basic toolkit and spare fan belt (one of each size required), radiator hoses and fuses, and a good tyre pump and pressure gauge (see Tyres & Pressures p61).

A set of jumper leads is also desirable, as well as a couple of litres of top-up engine oil, a bit of grease and a can of WD40. You can round off your basic kit with spare plugs, leads and points (if relevant), some electric wire, insulation tape and 'gaffer' tape, tie wire and zip-ties, and a small selection of bolts, nuts, washers and self-tapping screws.

Make sure the jack is in good working order, and don't forget a jacking plate to provide a base in the sand – a thick wooden plank will do. You 'll probably need this if you get stuck. Air-bag jacks work very well in sand, but carry one of these in addition to the standard jack, not instead of. A snatch strap with a couple of appropriately sized D-shackles can also come in handy.

A shovel or spade is useful for recovery as well as toilet functions. An axe may come in handy for building up a base of dead (never live) vege-tation under your wheels (see Getting Unstuck), though a bow saw might be easier to use.

Keep a pair of work gloves close at hand under the driver's seat for recovery work or for dirty jobs such as filling up with diesel. Finally, a dust-pan and brush will turn the daily chore of clear-ing sand out of the vehicle into a recurring joy.

Underbody car wash

Fuel

Fuel here is much more expensive than on the mainland, so fill up before you go across. The island is larger than you might think, however, and driving in soft sand – not to mention lower tyre pressures – can increase fuel consumption by up to 30% . There's a good chance you'll need a top-up.

Diesel and unleaded fuels are available at Kingfisher Bay, Eurong, Happy Valley, Cathedral Beach and Orchid Beach. Kingfisher Bay and Eurong now sell LPG gas too. At the time of research, Kingfisher didn't sell lead-replacement fuel as such but sold a lead additive in the shop.

Repairs & Towing

Limited emergency repairs are available at: Eurong, Ph (07) 4127 9173

Driving in Sand

The number one rule for driving in sand is to maintain momentum – not necessarily speed as such, but forward motion. The softer the sand, the more important this is. The moment you hesitate and ease off the accelerator and/or decide to shift down a gear in the middle of a difficult section, you're likely to be dragged to a stop (automatic transmissions offer advantages here). And once you've stopped, you can easily dig yourself in while trying to take off again.

So, if you see a daunting section coming up, line up the path you want to take (existing wheel tracks, preferably), maybe shift down a gear to ensure enough engine power, and stick to your guns till you're out the other end. It's always an exhilarating experience. Don't overdo it though, the trick is to floor the accelerator only when required and to stay in control.

High-ratio 4WD is usually best in sand. Low ratio doesn't provide enough momentum and tends to dig the vehicle in, though you may not have much choice if your engine lacks power, see how you go – youll soon find out. Low ratio may come in useful on steep downhill sections, or nursing the vehicle over Ngkala Rocks.

Always keep your thumbs outside or on the edge of the steering wheel. Existing wheel tracks can make it turn with incredible force, bruising or even breaking a thumb in the process.

safety issues

First-time visitors to Fraser Island don't always realise just how easily tyres can 'bite' into the sand – including the damp, hard-packed sand below the high-water mark on the eastern beach. A sudden change of direction can cause the front tyres to dig in and the vehicle to roll over before you know what's happening.

Rollovers are depressingly common on the beach. Sometimes they're the result of inexperienced drivers trying to show off, in which case they probably get what they deserve. Sometimes more noble causes are to blame, such as swerving to avoid a sudden obstacle. This can be another vehicle, a pedestrian who hasn't heard you coming over the roar of the surf, a sudden patch of soft sand, a freshwater creek with unexpectedly high banks, whatever. Take care and anticipate what may lie ahead so you can always drive smoothly and steer gradually. Check your mirrors so you don't deviate into the path of a vehicle that's overtaking you, and slow right down anywhere near people.

Also beware of the following:

- Consult the tide schedules in your *Fraser Island Information Pack* when driving along the beach, and note the subtleties of relatively low lows and high highs in the predicted water levels. Some sections of beach are impassable for one or two hours either side of high tide. In the south near Hook Point, for instance, the water comes right up to the steep dunes at high tide, so you're in real strife if your timing is wrong.
- Approach all creeks on the eastern beach with caution. They can gouge out deep channels with steep drop-offs that are often invisible until you're right at them. They vary from tide to tide, so what was shallow on the way up may be deep on the way back. They also tend to be deeper towards the dunes, so the closer you are to high tide, the bigger the risk. Slow down!
- Getting stuck in a water crossing is bad news, whether it's salt or fresh, as sand will wash away from underneath the wheels and the vehicle will sink to the body shell. Keep moving till you're back on the dry. If in doubt, don't even think about going in.
- There are several zones where small planes land on the beach. If encountering a moving plane, you usually need to drive high. The plane cannot manoeuvre as well as a vehicle in the softer sand. Slow down, drive high and wait for the plane to pass or stop.
- Never drive at night. Even at dusk, visibility can be dangerously low – patches of shiny coffee rock can seem like innocent puddles.
- Frontal collisions with other vehicles are a serious risk on the major tracks across the island – the Kingfisher-Eurong road, for instance. Stick to the 35km/hr speed limit and don't take any corner or crest for granted. On other tracks you may encounter nobody for ages and then get horribly caught out when you do!
- Keep to the left of oncoming vehicles. Only use indicators as you would on the mainland, for overtaking or turning.
- The roads can be very bumpy, so pack the vehicle carefully and if necessary tie luggage down so it doesn't fly through the cabin. A luggage barrier is well worth considering.

Incoming tide near Hook Point

Creek drop-offs can be a hazard

Tyres & Pressures

If maintaining momentum is the number one rule for driving in sand, low tyre pressures are number two. Lowering the pressure to about 60% or maybe even half of what's normal on bitumen presents a longer and wider 'footprint'. In most 4WDs this equates to 20-25psi, which helps keep the tyre on top of the sand and softens the power delivery. It also prevents 'hopping' and 'digging in' and minimises damage to the tracks.

Adjust the pressures before you drive off the ferry onto the island, as the sand in those very spots can be rather awful (of course, ensure you've engaged 4WD as well!).

Tyre types don't matter as much. You can have fun on large, wide 'desert' tyres (check with the manufacturer for correct pressures in sand), but even fairly narrow, truck-like tyres will handle sand just fine with low pressures.

Low pressures are not without risk, however. The longer contact areas and bulging sidewalls, which help your vehicle 'float' on top of the sand, attract sticks and other objects that can 'stake' a tyre, though Fraser Island is benign in this regard. High speeds on the eastern beach can also cause heat build-up leading to tread separation in an under-inflated tyre that's constantly flexing. And finally, you can easily peel a tyre off the rim with sharp or jerky steering. The lower the pressure, the more gradually you should steer and the slower and smoother you should drive.

Tube tyres can shift around the rim and rip out the valve if the pressure is too low and/or if your driving and braking forces are too high. The result will be an instant blowout. Tubeless tyres can also shift around the rim but not as easily, and it's not as disastrous if they do (although they may not seal properly afterwards).

If you're carrying a lot of weight in the vehicle, keep pressures at about 65% of what's normal on bitumen. The weight will make your tyres bulge enough anyway. If you're carrying little, it's still a good idea to keep a bit of pressure in reserve so you can let some air out as an emergency measure when you get stuck. Pressures as low as 15psi or even slightly lower can get you out of a lot of strife, but be wary of pressures below 15psi and don't forget to pump up the tyres again immediately afterwards.

It goes without saying that a reliable pump and tyre gauge are essential. So are valve caps, to prevent sand and salt entering the fragile valves. A couple of spare valves are a good idea too.

Don't forget to increase the tyre pressures again as soon as you return to terra firma after your visit.

Getting Unstuck

If you get stuck, don't panic, and don't keep spinning the wheels or you'll just dig yourself in further. Turning the wheel from side to side may improve traction a bit, but if that doesn't help get out of the vehicle and assess the situation. If it doesn't look like the underbody is resting firmly on the sand (yet), clear some sand away from the front and rear of the wheels and try rocking the vehicle back and forth by using reverse and first gear. Be gentle: you don't want to spin the wheels, just pack a small stretch of sand to provide a base from which you can take off (idling in low ratio may work well here).

Of course your passengers have disembarked by this stage in order to lighten the load, and you've ensured that 4WD is properly engaged. Passengers can help by pushing, but only if there are enough of them to make a difference (sand is a formidable anchor). A TroopCarrier with 10 backpackers has a distinct advantage here!

If this doesn't work, grab the shovel and clear away more sand, also from under the vehicle as much as possible (concentrate on the front and rear axles and differentials). Lower the tyre pressures a few psi (see the previous section). If this doesn't get you free, you've probably spun the wheels so deeply into the sand that the underbody is resting on the surface and the tyres will never get the traction they need.

Unfortunately there is no alternative now but to jack up each corner of the vehicle in turn and build up the surface under the tyres. Use the surrounding sand if nothing else is available, or otherwise wet sand from the beach or anything that provides a firm base – floor mats, dead branches or other vegetation (never live), anything else lying around. Do this properly, in stages if necessary by going back to each wheel a second time. Don't rush the job with half measures or it's likely you'll have to start all over again.

You should now be able to drive out, taking care to use just enough power to gain momentum without furiously spinning the wheels. Once you're moving, go for it!

If there's another vehicle to help out, you can save time by using the snatch strap, but only if your vehicle is not resting firmly on the sand. Otherwise the strap will just break, or the other vehicle will dig itself in too, or both.

A snatch strap is basically a huge elastic band that stores an enormous amount of energy, which makes it very effective in launching a vehicle that's stuck. But, it can be lethal if it breaks, even without a D-shackle attached, so make sure you know how to use it properly, and keep onlookers well away. Shake out the sand afterwards so it doesn't damage the webbing.

Transmission Wind-Up

If your vehicle has part-time 4WD (in other words, you have the option of engaging or disengaging 4WD), you should be aware of what's called transmission wind-up. If your vehicle has constant 4WD (in other words, the engine always transmits power to all four wheels), it's not an issue unless you lock the centre differential, which is a good idea in tricky sections (as well as turning off the traction control if fitted).

Make sure you know the 4WD setup in your vehicle and how to operate it. Many hire firms are a bit sloppy in explaining these sorts of things.

When you engage 4WD in a part-time 4WD or lock the centre diff in a constant 4WD, the front and rear axles lock together which can create tension in the transmission system. This is OK in soft sand or on rough tracks, where natural 'slippage' will alleviate the tension. On firm surfaces, however, the lack of 'slippage' can lead to transmission wind-up. You may begin to notice that the steering becomes a bit stiffer, but even if you don't, the tension in the transmission can increase to the stage where something breaks with a loud bang – which means the end of your trip and the beginning of a very expensive recovery-and-repair process.

Wind-up is surprisingly common on Fraser Island with its extremes of soft and hard surfaces. If your vehicle has part-time 4WD, disengage 4WD (or unlock the centre diff in a constant 4WD) on the eastern beach at low tide, the bitumen roads in Kingfisher Bay and Eurong, and the two gravel/dilapidated bitumen tracks in the south of the island. You don't have to unlock the front-wheel hubs as well (assuming you can on your vehicle), just disengage 4WD. If the 4WD lever seems stuck, and/or the 4WD light on the dashboard refuses to go out, you may already have slight transmission wind-up. Don't panic: simply reverse a few metres and all should be fine again (you may have to drive back and forth a few times).

Engaging 4WD and reducing tyre-pressure will help avoid getting bogged.

Using a jacking plate will help prevent the jack from sinking into the sand.

Driving at dusk can be dangerous

Remember to re-engage 4WD when you go back into the soft stuff, e.g. as you aim towards the dunes from the eastern beach. This author was not the first to get stuck because he forgot!

Vehicle Rentals

Toyota TroopCarriers with 10 backpackers are a common sight on the island, proof that renting a 4WD can be quite affordable if a few people get together to share expenses. You may pity the overloaded vehicle, but the occupants have a great time for a minimal outlay.

Make sure you rent a 'proper' 4WD that will handle the island easily (see What Type of 4WD). Daily rates drop significantly for longer term rentals, but there are many different deals and packages and your best bet is to ring around before making a decision.

The lowest rate is not necessarily the best – in fact, it often isn't. Read the small print carefully and check how many free kilometres are included, and what the insurance policy is, especially the excess which can be huge if a collision damage waiver is not included in the rate. Some vehicles come complete with camping gear, which is worth including in your calculations.

Also check whether the company actually allows you to take the vehicle onto the island. You can assume this is the case with local operators (though check anyway), but companies further afield often impose restrictions on where and how you may take their vehicles off the bitumen. Either way, it's highly unlikely that any company will let you take a vehicle north of Orchid Beach/Ocean Lake.

Make sure you know how the 4WD system works – some companies don't properly explain things like free-wheel hubs and low-ratio transmissions. They can also be a bit sloppy with vehicle preparation, so check the tyre pressures (including the spare), free-wheel hubs, standard toolkit, oil levels, windscreen washer reservoir etc.

Many people rent in Brisbane so they don't have to worry about getting to and from the island, but there are lots of hire firms in the area and on the island itself that can put you behind the wheel. If you rent locally, it is recommended that you choose a member of the Fraser Coast 4X4 Hire Association.

Check the following operators:

- **Australian 4WD-Hire**
  Ph 1300 360 339
  www.foorwheeldrivehire.net.au,
  australian4wdhire@bigpond.com.au
- **Aussie Trax 4x4 Rentals**
  Ph 1800 062 275, (07) 4124 4433
  www.fraserisland4wd.com.au,
  info@aussietrax.com.au
- **Bay 4 Wheel Drive Centre**
  Ph 1800 687 178, (07) 4128 2981
  www.bay4wd.com.au,
  info@bay4wd.com.au
- **Beachdrive 4WD Hire**
  Ph (07) 5447 2831, 0414 269 289
  othercar@optusnet.com.au
- **Fraser Island 4WD Taxi**
  Ph (07) 4127 9188, 0429 379 188
  www.fraserservice.com.au,
  enquiry@fraserservice.com.au
- **Fraser Magic 4WD Hire**
  Ph (07) 4125 6612
  www.fraser4wdhire.com.au,
  info@fraser4wdhire.com.au
- **Island Explorers 4WD Hire**
  Ph (07) 4124 3770
- **Kingfisher Bay 4WD Hire**
  Ph 1800 372 737
  www.kingfisherbay.com
- **Rainbow Beach Adventure Centre**
  Ph (07) 5486 3288
  www.adventurecentre.com.au
- **Safari 4WD Hire**
  Ph 1800 689 819, (07) 4124 4244,
  www.safari4wdhire.com.au,
  enquiry@safari4wdhire.com.au
- **Sargent Four Wheel Drive Hire Truck Lease & Rental**
  Ph 1800 077 353
  www.4wdhire.com.au

driving courtesy

Drive smoothly and carefully, and be considerate towards other drivers on the single-lane roads in the interior. Relax, you're here to enjoy yourself. Fraser Island etiquette includes the following:

- Small vehicles give way to large ones. It makes more sense for a LandCruiser to deviate into a passing bay than for a tour bus with 40 passengers. Similarly, lone vehicles give way to groups or those towing trailers.

- Vehicles going uphill give way to vehicles coming down. It's usually easier to back down to the last passing bay (or all the way downhill if necessary) than it is to reverse up.

- Check the rear-view mirrors occasionally in case a vehicle may wish to pass. They cannot do so on inland tracks unless you pull off the road.

- No-vehicle zones help provide some areas where walkers can safely enjoy a day on the beach without traffic hazards. These areas are demarcated with a large ship's rope stretching from the water's edge to the dunes. Do not drive into these areas.

Taxi

A 4WD taxi operates out of Eurong.
Ph (07) 4127 9188 or 0429 379 188,
www.fraserservice.com.au,
admin@fraser service.com.au
Bookings are essential.

Kingfisher Bay Resort also organises private 4WD tours where you determine what you want to see, but that's getting into tour territory (see Organised Tours p107).

Motorcycling

Motorcycles may soon be banned from the island, so check before you go.

Fraser Island's deep, soft sand is bad terrain for motorcycles, especially fully loaded. The few motorcyclists who come here report frequent spills. The eastern beach at low tide is great to ride on, but elsewhere you can't maintain the necessary momentum on the deeply rutted tracks that twist and turn.

If you must take a bike across, choose a fairly lightweight dual-purpose or enduro machine. If it doesn't look the part, the ferry captains will probably refuse you anyway.

Ideally it should have electric start (a dropped bike often floods and can be hellishly difficult to kickstart), and a large engine that produces lots of low-down 'grunt' that you'll really appreciate in sand. It must be roadworthy and fully registered, not just recreational-registered.

Getting Around

The only way to get around easily is by 4WD

ROB BOEGHEIM

Sand-riding techniques consist of moving back on the seat and maintaining momentum, shifting down a gear if necessary. Stand on the footpegs a bit to lower the centre of gravity and don't be afraid to let the bike 'wander' a little. Low tyre pressures certainly help. Don't try to 'jump ruts' unless they're shallow, and don't close the throttle. The latter will transfer weight onto the front wheel, causing it to dig into the sand, twist sideways and throw you over the bars. Good luck – you'll need it!

Weld a small steel plate to the bottom of the sidestand to prevent it sinking into the sand (or keep a flattened can or wooden plank handy). Make sure the clutch and brake levers can twist around the handlebars in a fall – if you do the clamps up tight, they'll break off. Apart from that, bring all the usual spares and a tyre pump, and wear good protective gear, especially solid boots (you'll be 'paddling' a lot with your legs, and they may get trapped under the bike when you fall).

The only positive thing about falling in sand is that the damage tends to be minor, even if the frequency of spills can wear you down and gradually wreck the bike.

Cycling

Forget it, though some hardy souls give it a go. The problems encountered on motorcycles are compounded on a bicycle as there's no engine to help maintain momentum. You have to be very fit, not because you'll be pushing the pedals hard but because you'll be pushing the bike a lot on the inland tracks (the hiking trails are off limits). Carry plenty of water.

A sturdy mountain bike or something similar with wide tyres is the only feasible choice for the sandy conditions. There's no bicycle shop on the island, so bring all the spares you think you'll need.

Coming in to land on the eastern beach

Walking

Quite a few people visit the island on foot, though not as many as could be expected with the beautiful hiking trails on offer. The trails and hikers' campsites are often empty and you might have them all to yourself. This is the great advantage of walking around Fraser Island as opposed to driving. And of course you see so much more!

There's no public transport to and from the ferry landings on the mainland or the island, which means hitching a ride or bracing yourself for a long slog. Roads on the island are very sandy and therefore tiring, but once you get onto the dedicated hiking trails the surface is harder and easier.

See Bushwalking pp 85-97 for more about walking, including descriptions of some of the longer hiking trails. There are also some short walks described in the What to See chapter.

Flying

You can fly to Fraser Island yourself – there are airstrips at Toby's Gap, Wanggoolba Creek, Orchid Beach and a 960x15m bitumen strip to the west of Eurong resort. Contact the airstrip managers and visitor information centres beforehand for more information.

Aircraft also use the ocean beach at Eurong, Eli Creek and Happy Valley – but only the commercial operators who know what they're doing. They offer joy flights that are quite affordable and provide an unforgettable, bird's-eye view of the island. Simply approach the pilots on the beach (if you can find them) or ring to make a booking.

The main operator is Air Fraser Island, which also connects Hervey Bay to Fraser Island daily. Helicopter services operate to and from Kingfisher Bay Resort. In the whale season, you can take whale-watch flights from Hervey Bay or Maroochydore (see Whale-Watching pp105-106).

- **Air Fraser Island**
  Ph (07) 4125 3600,
  www.airfraserisland.com.au, airfraser@bigpond.com
- **MI Helicopters**
  Ph (07) 4125 1599
  www.mihelicopters.com.au
- **Sunshine Aviation**
  Ph (07) 5450 0516
  www.sunshineaviation.com.au
  tours@sunshineaviation.com.au ■

Chapter Five

What To See

Fraser Island has an amazing number of sights packed into its relatively small area. You would need several weeks to do justice to them all, so we help narrow things down a bit with a selection of the major sights.

Central Station Area

Almost all visitors pass through Central Station at some stage, a major crossroads along the main track across the island. It's the most accessible area in which to experience the majestic rainforests of the central highlands.

Central Station (Map p122, E4)

Central Station itself is the starting point for several walks and tourist drives. Formerly known as Forest Station, it used to be the government's forestry headquarters and a busy little township. There's not much evidence of that today, though you can easily imagine why the residents would have preferred this site to the earlier one in the mosquito-infested, west-coast mangroves. Things can get busy when the tourist buses pull in around the middle of the day.

There's an interesting information bay next to the EPA office, along with a collection of relics from timber-cutting days, and an impressive array of massive staghorns on the surrounding trees. It's also a popular picnic and camping area. Gas barbecues are available in the picnic area, but bring your own fuel stove for the campground (no open fires allowed).

Staghorn with ribbon fern, Central Station

Left: Central Station   PHOTO: FRANK STOFFELS

Wanggoolba Creek (Map p122, E3)

Wanggoolba Creek at Central Station is one of the most photographed places on the island. It's not hard to see why, when within a few steps along the 450m boardwalk you've walked from an open, sunny picnic area into dark, lush rainforest seemingly miles from anywhere. The tall, straight trees in the former township suddenly give way to moss and lichen-covered logs, rainforest trees vainly shrugging off strangler figs, piccabeen palms, and the giant, prehistoric angiopteris ferns, which have the largest fern fronds in the world.

The water in the creek can be so clear and calm that it's hard to see (many first-time visitors have to look twice), and its white, sandy bed makes it almost silent. Stand still on the boardwalk and sniff the air. Listen to the rainforest sounds. You'll hear lizards rummaging through the leaf litter, birds calling to each other and the wind rustling the trees that line this magnificent creek.

The log bridging the creek takes you to a walking track that leads to Basin Lake (see page 70).

Pile Valley (Map p122, E4)

Pile Valley is home to awesome forest giants. Majestic satinay trees, many more than 40m tall, dwarf the palms and rainforest plants that share the valley. The place derives its name from the satinay piles that were used to refurbish the Suez Canal in the 1920s and London's docks after WWII.

Pile Valley

PETER DAVIS

Lake McKenzie

ROB BOEGHEIM

Lake McKenzie

FRANK STOFFELS

Lake Wabby

You can walk to Pile Valley from Wanggoolba Creek boardwalk at Central Station (2.4km, 50min). There's plenty of birdlife along the creek, including the occasional azure kingfisher. From Pile Valley you can return to Central Station back along the same track to Wanggoolba Creek boardwalk, or follow the track to complete the circuit through a hoop pine plantation. Return the same way or follow the vehicle track to an old logging track which winds through a hoop pine plantation back to Central Station (additional 2.2km, 50min). The Central Lakes Tourist Drive (red route) also passes through the valley.

The Lakes

Fraser Island has many lakes and streams unique to this environment that are of great scientific interest. See Geography & Habitats in the Backgrounds chapter for more about the different types of lakes. Most of the so-called perched lakes are in the central highlands to the north and south of Central Station, while most of the low-lying window lakes are in the far north of the island.

Lake McKenzie (Map p122, D4)

You'll be dazzled by your first glimpse of Lake McKenzie, the queen of the island's lakes. The sand that rings the lake is pure white and, as the lake gradually deepens, the water appears to turn an exotic shade of light blue. Then, the sandy shelf suddenly drops and the water changes to a deep, dark, bottomless blue though it's only 5-8m deep. The effect is mesmerising.

The lake is 130ha in area, sits 80m above sea level, and is probably the most picturesque example of a perched lake to be found anywhere. Not surprisingly, it is one of the island's most popular attractions and is best visited before 10am or after 2pm to avoid the tour buses and crowds. (If you want a pleasant lake swim away from the crowds, try Lake Birrabeen 5km to the south. It's just as nice as Lake McKenzie and may be quieter.)

There are several walks starting from Lake McKenzie including a 500m (20min) stroll to little McKenzie beach, a 6.3km (2hr 5min) walk via Basin Lake to Central Station, an 8km (3hr) walk via Pile Valley to Central Station, a 7km (2hr 30min) walk to McKenzies Jetty on the western beach, and an 8km (3hr) walk to Kingfisher Bay Resort. You can also walk to Kingfisher Bay along the western beach from McKenzies Jetty (30min) at low or mid tide.

Right: Lake McKenzie
FRANK STOFFELS

Basin Lake

Lake Birrabeen

Lake Boomanjin

Basin Lake (Map p122, E3)

This small, reed-fringed lake with its perfect shoreline is home to turtles and seven frog species (more than any other lake on the island). You can only get here on foot so it's often wonderfully peaceful even at the height of the tourist season. Reach the lake by walking from Central Station via the Wanggoolba Creek boardwalk (2km, 50min) or from Lake McKenzie (4.3km, 1hr 15min). Well worth the effort.

Lake Boomanjin (Map p124, A4)

Boomanjin (BOOM-an-jin) is the world's largest perched dune lake and one of Fraser's 'biggest' attractions. Unlike most other perched lakes, it is stream-fed. Its gleaming white sand shows through the honey-coloured water, the ripples in the sand creating wonderful patterns. Contorted melaleucas line the shore and, when the water level drops, a broader ring of white sand is exposed. A northern beach walk (2km, 45min) roams through the melaleucas and follows the Forest Lakes Trail markers back to the campground.

Lake Birrabeen (Map p122, F3)

This is a beautiful, crystal-clear lake with white sandy beaches similar to Lake McKenzie. It's less busy and therefore a great alternative to the battle for car parks and towel space. One of the highlights of the Central Lakes Tourist Drive, Lake Birrabeen has picnic facilities and a viewing platform, but no camping.

Lake Wabby & Hammerstone Sandblow (Map p123, E5)

Lake Wabby is a shrinking, dark-blue dot next to an immense yellow sandblow. Hammerstone Sandblow has dammed a creek to form Lake Wabby, and the steep sides of the sandblow have helped make this lake the deepest on the island (11m). The sandblow is creeping westward, gradually swallowing the lake and the surrounding forest, and in another 20 years Lake Wabby will be gone.

It was an important corroboree spot in Aboriginal times and is still classed as a 'women's place' by today's Butchulla.

You can see the lake and sandblow from the lookout off the Central Lakes Tourist Drive, or via a circuit walking track that leaves from a car park on the eastern beach 3.5km north of Eurong. (The walk is one-way along the track from the eastern beach into Lake Wabby, and two-way along the southern walking track.) A 4.7km return walk (1hr 50min) follows a ridge through coastal forests to the lake.

ROB BOEGHEIM

Ocean Lake

FRANK STOFFELS

Lake Allom (Map p121, D6)

This is a small but beautifully situated lake, with a picnic area tightly snuggled in vine forests, satinay and hoop pines. A circuit track (1.4km, 40min) leaves from the shady car park and ambles along the lake edge.

Ocean Lake (Map p117, F4)

This window lake sits behind the coastal fringe north of Orchid Beach and is the most northern place on the island with visitor facilities. The Cypress Circuit (20min, 1km) follows the lake's northern edge before swinging back to the car park, and shows an interesting range of local vegetation.

Eastern Beach

This part of the island, exposed to the prevailing south-easterly winds, offers many attractions and superb fishing spots that are easily reached by driving along the beach. For many visitors it epitomises what Fraser Island is all about.

Seventy-Five Mile Beach
(Maps p119, 121, 123, 124)

The beach itself is called Seventy-Five Mile Beach, even though it's 'only' 58 miles (92km) from Hook Point to Indian Head. It provides the quickest route for travelling the length of the island, and offers many attractions along the way – cliffs of coloured sand, several fresh-water creeks that flow across the beach, a large shipwreck, and a volcanic headland that is visible through the salty haze from many kilometres away. Fishing in the surf gutters is excellent, but unfortunately the fierce rips and cruising sharks make it totally unsuitable for swimming or surfing.

Most tourists stick to the section between Eurong and Happy Valley, though many also continue on to Indian Head. If you want peace and quiet to really appreciate the majesty of this beach, head for the section south of Dilli Village where the only passing vehicles are those travelling to/from the ferry at Hook Point.

Driving along the beach on Fraser's East Coast

FRANK STOFFELS

What To See

Bear in mind, though, that the beach gets narrower the further south you go, and at high tide the water can come right up to the dunes near Hook Point. In that case, the dilapidated bitumen road along the inland side of the dunes (a former sand-mining road) presents a safe alternative.

About 11km north of Eurong, Poyungan Rocks present an obstacle at high tide as well. The bypass track is a bit rough, so if you have a choice, time your arrival for the lower end of the tide so you can simply drive around them.

Seventy-Five Mile Beach

Rainbow Gorge (Map p123, C6)

A 1.9km (1hr) circuit track from the beach leads through a cypress forest to this small gorge of red, yellow, white and brown sands. Don't climb on them as they are very fragile. They're not as spectacular as the Pinnacles further north (see page 75), but the walk back to the car park across the impressive Kirrar Sandblow makes up for it.

About 2.5km north of Rainbow Gorge, Yidney Rocks are impassable at high tide and the bypass track (which also leads to Happy Valley) is a bit rough, but at low tide you can simply drive around them.

ROB BOEGHEIM

Poyungan Rocks

Eli Creek

Eli Creek (Map p121, F6)

This is the largest creek on the eastern beach and pours up to four million litres of clear, fresh water into the ocean every hour. It's a popular picnic and swimming spot, with a boardwalk that follows the creek inland through banksia and pandanus (some sections of the boardwalk may be closed for reconstruction). Swimming or floating down the swiftly flowing creek from the bridge at the far end of the boardwalk is an invigorating experience.

Take care when driving through the creek on the beach, as its fast-flowing water can gouge out deep channels. At high tide it's best to take a break and go for a swim until you can cross the creek at the lower end of the beach.

ROB BOEGHEIM

Floating down Eli Creek

ROB BOEGHEIM

Maheno Wreck (Map p121, E6)

On the beach between Eli Creek and The Pinnacles is the landmark wreck of the *Maheno*, a trans-Tasman passenger liner that also served as a hospital ship in WWI. Sold for scrap metal to Japan, it was being towed northwards on 9 July 1935 when an unseasonable cyclone hit. The tow cable broke and it was driven high onto the beach by the wind and waves.

Efforts to refloat it were unsuccessful, but it served a useful purpose in WWII when the air force used it for target practice, and the island's Z-Force commandos practised their ship-boarding and limpet-mining skills on the hulk.

After many decades of pounding waves and corroding salt, the wreck is just a sinking, crumbling, rusting relic of its former self and is now unsafe. Access is prohibited within 3m of the wreck.

Wear shoes, as rusty, jagged metal protrudes from the sand. Park on the upper beach (but not on the vegetation) and watch for through traffic – you may not hear oncoming cars over the sound of surf and wind. Stay with your children at all times.

The informative display board on the upper beach is well worth a read, but also take a look at the old *Maheno* photographs inside the Satinay Bar & Bistro at Happy Valley, or the central complex of the Kingfisher Bay Resort, to gain a true appreciation of the power of the elements. You can see one of the ship's typically deep bathtubs among the forestry memorabilia at Central Station.

As well as being a lonely, poignant sight, the stark, rusty colours mean great photos, especially when the *Maheno* glows red with the sunset.

'Maheno' Wreck

ROB BOEGHEIM

The Pinnacles (Map p121, E7)

The coloured sand formations at the Pinnacles are quite impressive. Wind and rain have eroded the sand mass, exposing the underlying, harder sands and moulding them into spectacular sculptures. Iron oxides provide bright streaks of red and orange. They're best viewed and photographed in the early morning sun, when the vibrant gold sands look fantastic against a deep-blue sky.

The Cathedrals (Map p121, C7)

The coloured sand cliffs culminate in the Cathedrals, which stretch the full length of Cathedral Beach and provide a dramatic backdrop for an ocean beach drive, walk or fishing expedition. One of the more spectacular sections includes **Red Canyon** with its deep reds and ochres, 3km north of Dundubara.

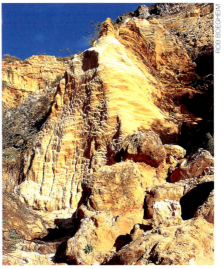

The Pinnacles

Red Canyon

North of Red Canyon the beach gets narrower, and about 10km south of Indian Head the water meets the dunes at high tide, so check the tide schedules before heading up here.

The view from Indian Head is awesome

Indian Head viewed from the north

Indian Head & Waddy Point Area

You could say that this rocky area is the 'birthplace' of Fraser Island. Along with Middle Rocks and other outcrops at Boon Boon Creek on the west coast, they're the only true rocks on the island (remnants of an ancient volcano), and it was here that sand carried north from the New England Tablelands first began accumulating some 800,000 years ago.

Indian Head (Map p119, E6)

The largest rock formation on the island was named by Captain Cook as he sailed past in May 1770, because he saw the campfires of the local inhabitants who were then referred to as Indians. It is still held under native title.

It's a short walk to the top and the view is well worth the effort (the trails are not constructed tracks and contain hazards, so take care). You can often see manta rays, sharks, dolphins and whales in the sea below. Stay with your children and keep well back from cliff edges – one person has already fallen to their death here.

The bypass track around Indian Head consists of deep, soft sand that can trap the unwary.

The Champagne Pools at high tide

Champagne Pools (the Aquarium) (Map p119, D6)

The Champagne Pools north of Indian Head, at the southern end of Middle Rocks, are natural fish traps that were used by the Aboriginal people. Waves crashing over the rock wall create the 'champagne bubbles' for which they are named. It's the only spot where you can swim along the eastern beach, but only at low tide as the water really rips through here at other times.

Reach the pools via a 350m boardwalk from the southern car park or walk a similar distance from the northern (or Middle Rocks) car park. You can also walk 4km (1hr 30min) down from Waddy Point along South Waddy Beach.

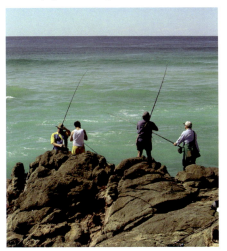

Fishing at Waddy Point

Middle Rocks

Middle Rocks (Map p119, D6)

Lookouts at Middle Rocks reward you with spectacular views south toward Indian Head, north towards Waddy Point, and east out across the ocean where whales and dolphins can be seen. The beaches in this area between Indian Head and Waddy Point are more sheltered than the other ocean beaches and are favoured by fishers.

Waddy Point (Map p119, D6)

This rocky outcrop is also a great fishing spot, and the sheltered waters north of here allow boats to be launched safely. Just inland to the north is a ranger station and a EPA campground with facilities, though many fishers prefer to camp on the beach. Beware of sharks attracted to the bait and offal.

Binngih Sandblow (Map p119, D5)

The top of Binngih Sandblow behind Waddy Point ("Binngih" is the Aboriginal name for Waddy Point) offers magnificent views of Sandy Cape, Marloo Bay and Waddy Point.

The Binngih circuit track (750m, 25min) starts behind Waddy Point campground and treks through coastal woodland to the sandblow. Return along the same track, or head 800m down the sandblow to North Waddy Beach and stroll 1km (15min) along the beach to the campground. You can also cross Binngih Sandblow to reach South Waddy Beach and the start of the walk to Champagne Pools. Beware of the slippery rocks – walk in groups and stay with your children.

What To See

The North & Sandy Cape

The north of Fraser Island is remote, with far fewer visitors than the rest of the island. It's a true wilderness area. You're almost guaranteed a solitary visit because of the tricky rock negotiations, the deep, soft sand, the tide restrictions, and total lack of facilities.

The landscape is also different with more exposed sand and less vegetation, giving the area an arid, desert-like feel. There are immense sandblows that remind you that the island is all sand – something you easily forget when walking through the lush, forested areas further south.

There are no tracks in the interior and vehicles can only travel along the beach from Orchid Beach up to Sandy Cape and around to Flinders Sandblow and the lighthouse (the turtle rookery beyond here is a no-go area). The route is suitable only for well set-up vehicles with experienced drivers, who are advised to travel in convoy. Rental vehicles are not allowed north of Orchid Beach/Ocean Lake (see the earlier Lakes section). Hikers must be experienced and well prepared, and due to the lack of established trails, the going can be slow. Water can be harder to find here than in other parts of the island.

Ngkala Rocks

Ngkala Rocks (Map 117, E4)

This outcrop of coffee rock forms the main vehicular hazard between Waddy Point and Sandy Cape. A sandy bypass track is the only option around South Ngkala Rocks but has bogged countless vehicles in its deep, soft sand. The track returns to the beach where the rough and slippery North Ngkala Rocks offer the next obstacle. Make sure you arrive here exactly at low tide.

Flinders Sandblow

Sandy Cape (Map 117, A4)

Sandy Cape is Fraser's most northern point above the waterline. A sandbar known as **Breaksea Spit** stretches underneath the water from Sandy Cape for 35km. The cape feels far removed from the rest of the island and is a tranquil spot to fish or watch the colliding currents.

Left: Sandy Cape FRANK STOFFELS
Flinders Sandblow

Flinders Sandblow (Map 117, A3)

The sandblow has a steep northern side and is like the leading edge of the island, continuously pushing north with the wind and ocean currents. The views from atop the sandblow are marvellous: turquoise waters, gentle waves and an ocean that falls over the horizon.

Sandy Cape Lighthouse (Map p117, A4)

The lighthouse was constructed in 1870 due to the growing number of shipwrecks in the area. The walk to the lighthouse is a steep 1.2km. Other short walks (one way) from the entry include a 1.3km (20 min) walk to the graves of the first lighthouse keeper and his daughter, and 600m (10 min) to WWII bunkers.

West Coast

This is the lee side of the island and its make-up is markedly different to the continuous beach/dune stretch along the east coast. The many estuaries and mangroves, especially south of Moon Point facing the sheltered waters of Great Sandy Strait, provide a fascinating variety of land forms, vegetation and fauna. Sand flies can be a major nuisance though, so come prepared.

Vehicles are only allowed on the beach between Moon Point and Wathumba Creek, but the potential hazards are many and driving here is only advisable for those with experience in well set-up vehicles. The leached white sand is softer than along the east coast and will easily bog a vehicle. The stunningly beautiful beach is narrower too, so keep a very close eye on tide schedules. There are several potentially treacherous creek crossings (Coongul Creek in particular) with bottomless mud and deep weed banks covered with a shallow layer of sand, appearing to offer a safe driving surface. The latter can be very hard to spot, but they occur on the upper part of the beach at creek crossings. Always test your route across a creek on foot before driving through.

Platypus Bay (Map p117-118, D1)

The beaches of Platypus Bay are closed to vehicular traffic, but a particularly beautiful section of beach is accessible by walking along the 10km management track from Orchid Beach township. The calm, clear waters play upon the white sands and offer one of the few quiet swimming spots away from the perils of the ocean beaches. There's little or no shade and no facilities.

Wathumba Creek (Map p118, D3)

Wathumba Creek is the most northern campground with facilities on the western beach. The estuary is a popular yacht anchorage and is also popular with mosquitoes and sand flies, so bring plenty of repellent. The sunsets here are magnificent.

Paddling on Wathumba Creek

FRANK STOFFELS

What To See

ROB BOEGHEIM

Sandy Cape Lighthouse

Wathumba Creek at sunset

What To See

Aerial view of Wathumba Creek (looking south)

The beach south of Wathumba is swampy and treacherous and Wathumba Creek itself is impossible to cross. Some foolhardy folk have tried and lost their vehicles in the process. The beach from Wathumba Creek north to Sandy Cape Lighthouse is a 'No Vehicle Zone'. The only safe land route to Wathumba is via a track from Orchid Beach which skirts along the **Wathumba Swamp**. The swamp is one of the largest on the island and is another example of Fraser's diversity.

Platypus Bay

Moon Point

Deep Creek logging ramp

McKenzies Jetty (Map p122, D3)

Logs and sawn timber from Fraser's only sawmill (established 1918) were shipped from McKenzies Jetty (built 1919) to the mainland. The McKenzie enterprise soon pulled out but the forestry department continued to operate the jetty till 1937. Its remains are a great photographic object, especially at sunset.

A walking track just north of the creek crossing at the jetty leads inland to the former township of **Balarrgan** (North White Cliffs). This was a quarantine station from 1872 to 1896, and briefly an Aboriginal mission at the turn of the century. In the first decades of the 20th century it was a sawmill and logging township consisting of 30 shacks and a school. In WWII it was a military training camp, but little remains today. Return to the beach along the same path or, if driving, follow the vehicle track north to Kingfisher Bay.

The South-West (Maps p122 & 124)

Below the Wanggoolba Creek ferry landing, the southern quarter of the west coast gets few visitors yet it offers a variety of natural attractions and some great fishing spots.

One of these is **Ungowa**, with its condemned jetty, which was the island's forestry headquarters in the final days of logging. The campground here has limited facilities but is a good base for estuarine fishing and for exploring the nearby fens.

Just south of here is **Deep Creek**, a great picnic spot and camping site with commanding views from the South White Cliffs. Down beneath are the remains of an old logging ramp. Slightly further south again, **Buff Creek** is similar.

Then there's **Garrys Anchorage**, the southernmost point on the west coast that you can easily reach by vehicle. As the name implies, it's a popular anchorage for private yachts, but it also has a pleasant campground with very limited facilities.

The road beyond here down to Hook Point is not maintained, and further progress may be barred by fallen trees and other vegetation. Technically the road is not all that challenging, and if the rangers have just been through with their chainsaws it presents an interesting (if slow) alternative route to/from the southern ferry landing. Because of the isolation, it is recommended that you travel in convoy. ■

What To See

Chapter Six

What To Do

Three days will give you a taste of the best of Fraser Island, but you'll want more time to really appreciate and enjoy the numerous attractions. A good way to do that is to engage in one or more of the many activities for which the island is justly famous.

Bushwalking

Much of the island's unique flora and fauna only reveals itself when you go walking, and the place is a bushwalker's paradise. There are over 40 trails to choose from and most are easy with gentle gradients, if a bit sandy at times.

Some of the shorter trails have already been described in the previous chapter under the relevant sights to which they are attached. Most are well within the scope of the casual walker. Following is a selection of the longer walks including the Fraser Island Great Walk, that require a reasonable level of fitness and, in some cases, preparation with camping gear etc as they can take several days to complete.

The most important equipment is a good pair of walking shoes that have already been 'broken in'. Sand in shoes will chafe and lead to blisters, so shake them out when you take a break. Gore-Tex or similar types of water-repellent linings are easily damaged by sand – check for sand under the insoles.

Beware of sunburn, so avoid the midday sun and always wear a hat, sunglasses and long-sleeved shirt. Many walkers prefer shorts, but comfortable tracksuit pants are worth considering and will minimise scratches from the dense scrub in some areas. Preferably walk in a group, and carry a stick for snakes, spider webs and dingoes. Maps are essential (the ones in this book should generally suffice) and a compass will definitely help. Take plenty of water, and boil water from lakes and streams before drinking (it's usually OK as is but you can't be sure).

Stay on the tracks – in the event of bushfire (an occasional risk on the island), rangers will only check designated tracks and camping sites. When walking along the beach, beware of vehicles which often are hard to hear over the roar of the surf.

Left: Beach fishing. FRANK STOFFELS

Before starting any overnight walk in the dry season, check fire restrictions or track closures by contacting the Eurong EPA office, Ph (07) 4127 9128. Always inform someone reliable back home of your intended route and completion date. Stick to your plans or let them know of changes, and don't forget to check in again at the end of your trip.

Refer to the Short Walks brochure that comes with your Fraser Island Information Pack. The EPA offices also stock a low-cost Forest Lakes Trail brochure that describes each of the walks that make up this trail, along with a wealth of information on the flora and fauna of the island. A Fraser Island Great Walk topographic map is available (ph 07 3227 8185 for stockists). Also see the Camping section in the Where to Stay chapter of this book for advice on where and how to camp.

Finally, some advice on transport. Many of the trails are linear, going from A to B rather than back to A, which raises the question of how to get there and back. Some people hitchhike, which is easy on this friendly island so long as you're not in a group carrying huge packs. Others arrive here in a group with one or more vehicles to begin with, in which case it's simple to organise a drop-off and pick-up. The resorts may also be willing to help if you're staying there. And of course there's always the taxi at Eurong, Ph (07) 4127 9188 or 0429 379 188, so long as you can find a phone or get a connection on your mobile. Even so, you'll probably find that the taxi is busy, so it's best to book in advance.

Seabirds

ROB BOEGHEIM

Wungul Sandblow Circuit

5.5km (2hr), moderate

Starting from the western end of Dundubara campground, the track climbs up onto the medium-sized sandblow (great sea views) and then turns west over the sandblow. Cool off on the walk back through the tall eucalypt forests and either cut across via the firebreak walk to the campground or continue towards the beach.

The sandblow is very exposed to the sun, so wear protection and avoid the middle of the day.

Bowarrady Trail

11km one way (3hr 15min), moderate

Leave the ocean beach and walk through tall eucalypt forest past the Wungul Sandblow before heading through swampland and vine thickets. Sit by the lake and watch the wildlife before returning along the same track or staying at the hikers' camp at nearby **Lake Geeoong**. About 2km south of **Lake Bowarrady** is 244m Mt Bowarrady, the island's highest point.

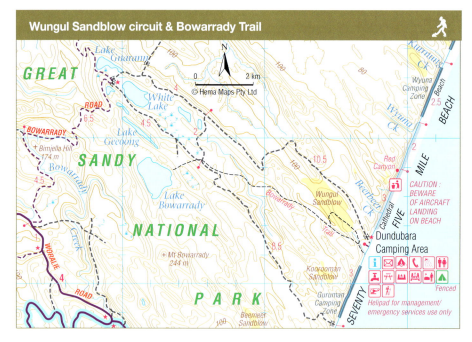

Wungul Sandblow

Forest Walk via Lake Coomboo & Hidden Lake

12.4km one way (3hr 15min), moderate

This is one of the more rewarding walks on the island. Start at the car park just off the Northern Forests Tourist Drive and if possible send a driver to the other end of the walk to meet you. Walk past the banksia woodland and pretty eucalypt forest towards **Lake Coomboo**. After taking a break at its dark waters, retrace your steps about 500m from the lake and turn south.

The track past **Hidden Lake** takes you through many of the island's distinctive forest types including eucalypt forest, blackbutt forest, vine forests of satinay and brush box, rainforest and carrol thickets. The vegetation is so thick that Hidden Lake itself isn't visible from the track. Keep walking south, leaving the cool rainforest gully for an easy climb along an old logging track to more banksia woodland and eucalypt forest, then meet up again with the Northern Forests Tourist Drive.

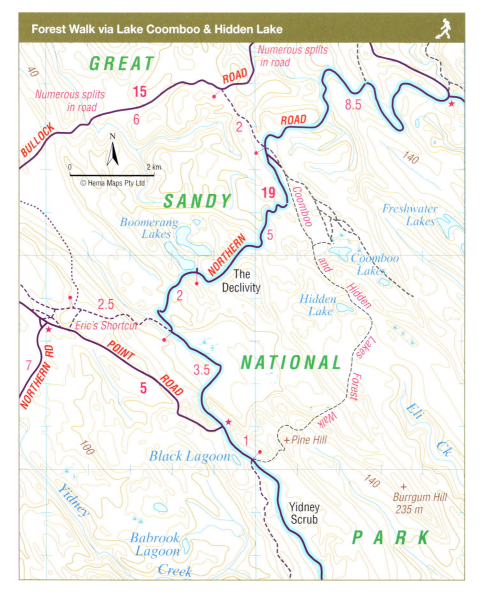

Forest Walk via Lake Coomboo & Hidden Lake

What To Do

Forest Lakes Trail

This trail joins many of the short walks, has six sections and takes four to six days to complete. The individual sections take half a day to a day each, depending on your walking speed and how long you spend at the various attractions. A low-cost and highly recommended brochure describing the trail in detail is available from the ranger stations and the EPA offices in Maryborough and Rainbow Beach.

Section 1:
Lake McKenzie to Central Station
*6.3km one way (2hr),
moderate to challenging*

Leave Lake McKenzie and meander south along the high central dunes through tall eucalypt forests, vine forests, open woodland, heath and carrol (grey myrtle) thickets to **Basin Lake**, then towards the rainforest gully of Wanggoolba Creek and Central Station.

If you wish, you can tack on a return walk to **Pile Valley** (2.4km, 50min) – see Pile Valley p67.

Another Route
Lake McKenzie to Central Station
8 km one way (3hr), moderate

Alternatively, you can leave Lake McKenzie in the direction of Lake Wabby instead, along Section 6 of the Forest Lakes Trail, for approximately 3km before turning south towards Pile Valley along an old tramline route (walk 15b in the Short Walks brochure that comes with your Fraser Island Information Pack), and from there to Central Station.

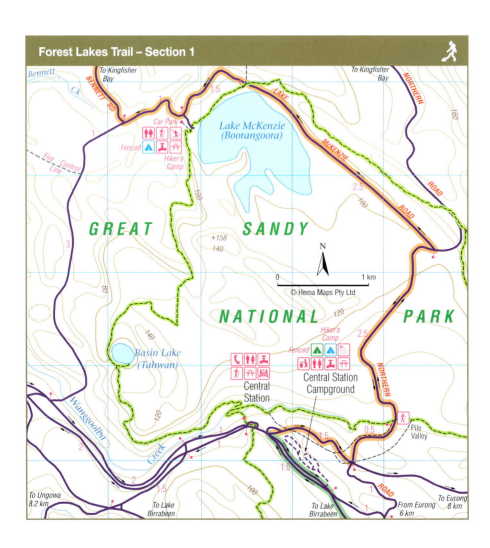

FRANK STOFFELS

Boardwalk to Lake McKenzie

Lake Benaroon

Forest Lakes Trail
Section 2: Central Station to Lake Benaroon Hikers' Camp
7.3km one way (2hr 20min), moderate

Continue south through the shady, tall eucalypt forests, which are decorated with vines, epiphytes and carrol understorey, along the ridges towards **Lake Jennings** and **Lake Birrabeen**. Both are worth a look. Pass near Birrabeen's eastern shore and continue through open heath past **Barga Lagoon** (also known as Lake Barga) to Lake Benaroon hikers' camp.

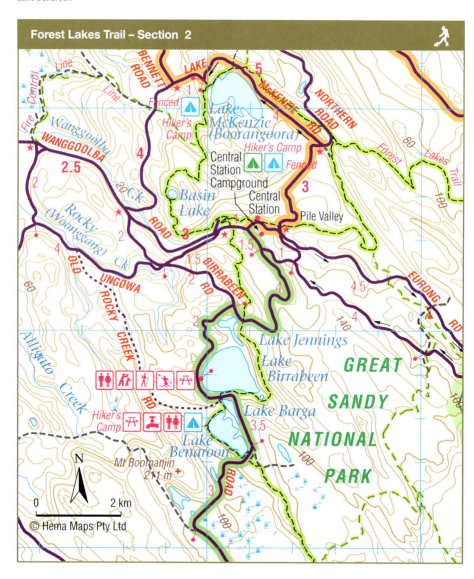

Forest Lakes Trail – Section 2

© Hema Maps Pty Ltd

What To Do

Lake Birrabeen is always much quieter than Lake McKenzie.

Forest Lakes Trail
Section 3: Lake Benaroon Hikers' Camp to Lake Boomanjin
7.3km one way (2hr 30min), easy

Leave the camp and continue along the lakeshore briefly before turning southeast. Walk through tall, closed eucalypt forest, carrol thickets and rainforest, then along ridges flourishing with scribbly gum and blackbutt woodlands before descending into a dense carrol thicket. After the thicket, catch glimpses of the ocean through airy woodlands. Descend towards Lake Boomanjin and cross the northern shore to the campground.

Lake Boomanjin

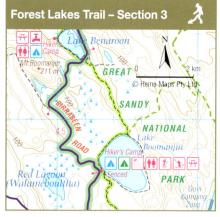
Wildlife is in abundance at the Lakes

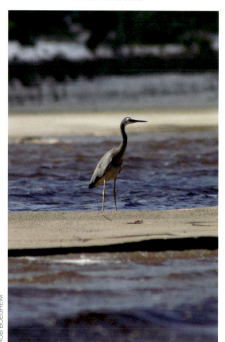

Foxtail

Forest Lakes Trail
Section 4: Lake Boomanjin to Dilli Village
6.3km one way (2hr 20min), moderate to challenging

Leave Lake Boomanjin and continue along the ridges through tall trees then woodland filled with foxtail sedge, grass trees and ferns. Skirt around **Wongi Sandblow**, enjoy the wide views, and descend towards Dilli Village across coastal wetlands.

What To Do

Forest Lakes Trail
Section 5: Dilli Village to Lake Wabby
17.3km one way (5hr 30min),
difficulty depends on tide and winds

Leave Dilli Village and head north along the ocean beach. Beware of vehicles – their noise gets drowned out by the roar of the surf. At **Eurong**, drop into the bakery for fresh pastries and continue back along the beach to the second Lake Wabby beach entrance. Cross over the coastal dunes into a rainforest filled with melaleucas, cypress trees and vines before reaching the edge of **Hammerstone Sandblow**. Cross over the sandblow towards Lake Wabby.

Lake Wabby

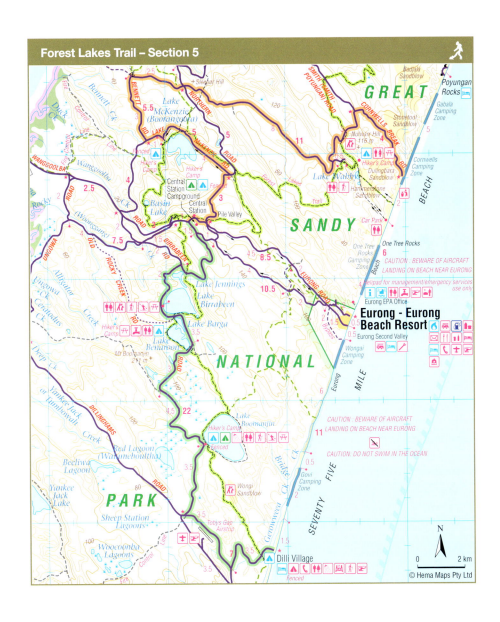

© Hema Maps Pty Ltd

Forest Lakes Trail
Section 6:
Lake Wabby to Lake McKenzie
11.9km one way (3hr 30min), moderate

Leave the lake's edge and climb up to the Lake Wabby lookout for a tremendous view. Heading south, the trail wanders through open forest, which becomes taller the further inland you travel, then makes way for vine forest with kauri pine, lilly-pilly trees, palm lilies and vines. As the track rises, the rainforest disappears and you're back in carrol and tall eucalypt country. The last section of the trail continues to beautiful Lake McKenzie.

Sandblow vegetation helps stabilise the shifting dunes

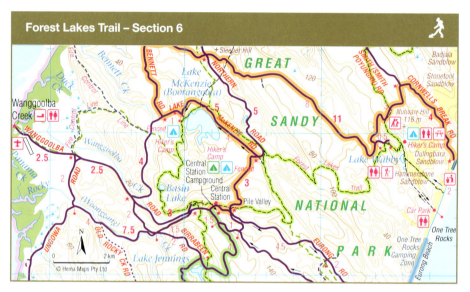

Lake McKenzie

What To Do

Fraser Island Great Walk
(Map p122-124)

The Fraser Island Great Walk is one of six world-class walking tracks being developed by the Queensland government to promote some of the most beautiful areas in the state, including three of its World Heritage Areas. The Fraser Island version provides a continuous track from Dilli Village to Lake Garawongera (near Happy Valley), passing some of the island's most famous landmarks. Its total length is 85km and should take six to eight days to walk.

A topographic map of the walk is available, and EPA advises all walkers to carry it.

The walk is broken up into four sections, with walker-only camping sites spaced at four to five-hour intervals. The first two sections follow the existing Forest Lakes Trail, with upgrades, realignments and several new camping sites. The last two sections are entirely new and open up some of the island's most impressive rainforest areas.

The walk is designed so that hikers can choose between short walks, full-day walks, overnight walks and two to three-day walks, with signposts leading to a number of excursions along the way.

There are also many feeder routes providing access to the Great Walk.

Section 1: Dilli Village to
Central Station (Map p122-124)

Leaving Dilli Village head up to skirt around Wongi Sandblow, enjoying the wide views. Continue along the ridges through woodland filled with foxtail sedge, grass trees and ferns then tall trees to Lake Boomanjin. [6.3km, 2-3hr]

From Lake Boomanjin head towards Lake Benaroon hikers' camp through dense carrol thicket and along ridges flourishing with scribbly gum and blackbutt woodlands before reaching tall closed eucalypt forest, carrol thickets and rainforest. [7.2km, 2.5-3.5hr]

From Lake Benaroon, continue past Barga Lagoon through open heath. Then walk through the shady tall eucalypt forests, which are decorated with vines, epiphytes and carrol understorey, along ridges towards Lake Birrabeen and Lake Jennings and then down to Central Station. [7.5km, 2.5-3.5hr]

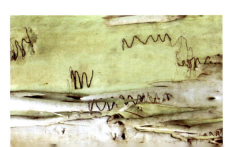

Wanggoolba Creek

TOURISM QUEENSLAND

What To Do

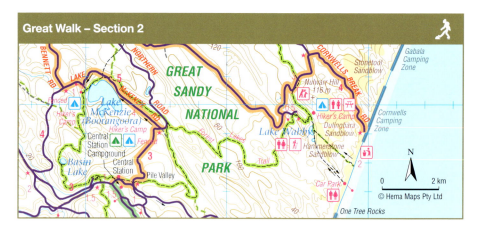

Section 2: Central Station to Lake Wabby (Map p122-123)

In this section there are two options, either go directly to Lake Wabby through Pile Valley or via Basin Lake and Lake McKenzie. To complete the latter, from Central Station head past Basin Lake through tall eucalypt forests, vine forests, open woodland, heath and carrol thickets to Lake McKenzie. To go via Pile Valley, follow the Wanggoolba Creek boardwalk through the rainforest gully before heading on towards Lake Wabby. [6.6km, 3-4hr or via Pile Valley 11.3km, 3.5-4.5hr]

From the beautiful Lake McKenzie, the track continues through carrol and tall eucalypt country before heading into vine forest, with kauri pine, lilly-pilly trees, palm lilies and vines. The vine forest opens into tall forest, wandering to Lake Wabby and its lookout with tremendous views. [11.9km, 4-5hr]

Section 3: Lake Wabby to Valley of the Giants (Map p123)

After Lake Wabby, the track re-enters closed forest before following a ridge that provides great views over the Badjala Sandblow. The Valley of the Giants is a real highlight of the Great Walk. This magnificent rainforest valley contains some of the island's largest living trees, and has only recently been reopened to the public. [16.2km, 5.5-7.5hr]

Lake Wabby

ROB BOEGHEIM

What To Do

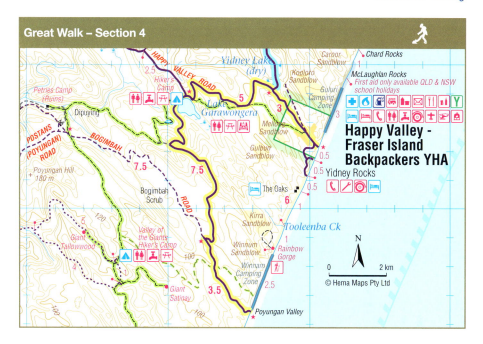

Great Walk – Section 4

Chard Rocks
Caroor Sandblow
Yidney Lake (dry)
Kooloro Sandblow
McLaughlan Rocks
* First aid only available QLD & NSW school holidays
Guluri Camping Zone
HAPPY VALLEY ROAD
2.5
Hiker's Camp
Petries Camp (Ruins)
Dipuying
Lake Garawongera
5
3
Happy Valley - Fraser Island Backpackers YHA
POSTANS (POYUNGAN) ROAD
BOGIMBAH ROAD
7.5
7.5
Mellong Sandblow
Gulbun Sandblow
0.5
0.5
0.5
Yidney Rocks
Poyungan Hill 180 m
Bogimbah Scrub
The Oaks
6
1
Kirra Sandblow
Tooleenba Ck
Valley of the Giants Hiker's Camp
Giant Tallowwood
Winnum Sandblow
Rainbow Gorge
1
N
Winnum Camping Zone
2.5
0   2 km
© Hema Maps Pty Ltd
3.5
Giant Satinay
Poyungan Valley

Section 4: Valley of the Giants to Lake Garawongera (Map p123)

After spending some time in the Valley of the Giants, continue through giant brushbox and satinay forests then along Bogimbah Creek to historic former logging camps. From Lake Garawongera you can follow an additional 6.6km (2.5-3.5hr) walk along a steep ridge then through open forest to Happy Valley. [13.1km, 4.5-6.5hr]

Driving

Driving around the island is always a bit of an adventure. However, people who come here to indulge their rally-driving fantasies and churn up this valuable and fragile place in their 4WDs are thoughtless in the extreme. Driving here is best seen as a way of getting to the many sights and relaxing activities. The What to See chapter provides some driving options in this respect. The Getting Around chapter addresses sand driving and vehicle rentals.

Many of Fraser Island's best features and walking tracks are linked by four, colour-coded tourist drives. They are easy to follow using the coloured roadside markers and are a pleasant way to see the attractions. Each of these drives will fill a morning or afternoon, but they are short enough that you'll be able to allocate generous time to the short walks and attractions along the way.

Yidney Scrub

Northern Forests Tourist Drive (Blue)

37.5km, 2.5hr driving time

Turn into Woralie Road just south of **the Pinnacles** (the sign there says "Woralie Track") and climb up alongside Knifeblade Sandblow. Detour 400m off the drive to a car park and wander past large scribbly gums to the **Knifeblade Lookout** (260m, 6min). You'll see grey skeletons of trees exposed by the trailing edge of the sandblow as it continues its voracious march across the forest.

Continue the drive to **Lake Allom**, which hides among the tall trees. The route then swings southwest through banksia woodland and heads past **the Declivity**, a surprisingly large, deep depression on the eastern side of the road. The Lake Coomboo & Hidden Lake forest walk starts about 1km before the Declivity (see p87).

On the opposite side of the road a little further on are the **Boomerang Lakes**, the highest dune lakes in the world (130m above sea level). After a walk along an old vehicle track to the lake edge (530m, 12min), head southeast through **Yidney Scrub** – a rainforest filled with kauri pines – towards Happy Valley.

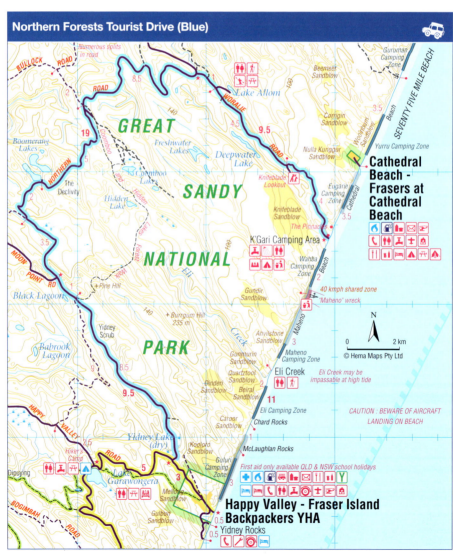

Lake Garawongera Tourist Drive (Yellow)

19km, 1hr driving time

This is the shortest of the drives but it is very scenic. Leave Happy Valley and head through some beautiful rainforest to **Lake Garawongera**, which is a popular swimming spot and picnic area. The dark-blue lake is lined with reeds and melaleucas and is a great place for quiet reflections. After an enjoyable stopover, continue through tall forests and open woodland to Poyungan Valley and the ocean.

Lake Garawongera

Rainforest

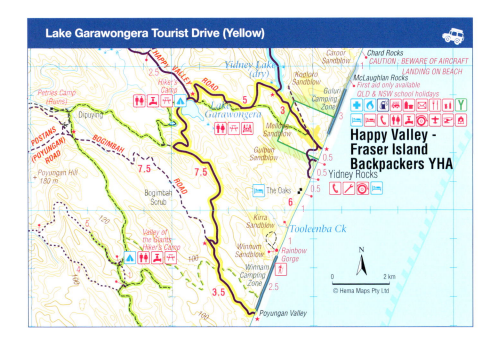

Central Lakes Tourist Drive (Red)

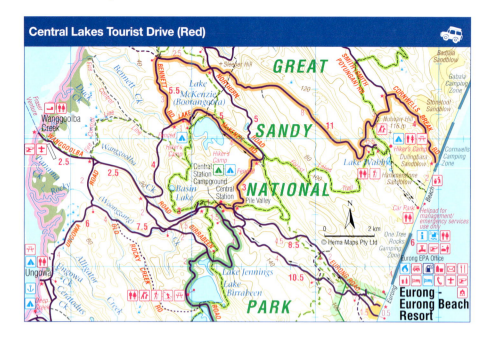

Southern Lakes Tourist Drive (Green)

Central Lakes Tourist Drive (Red)

28.5km, 2hr driving time

This drive starts near Central Station and then dips and winds north through dark, shady forests. It passes the coarse-barked giants of **Pile Valley** before skirting around **Lake McKenzie**.

Further on, the drive passes the turnoff to **Lake Wabby Lookout**, where a 10min stroll (400m) awards you with a spectacular view across Lake Wabby, **Hammerstone Sandblow**, and the dark, green forests to the ocean. You can opt for a closer look and perhaps a cool dip in Lake Wabby, or return to your vehicle to continue the drive.

The next diversion is **Stonetool Sandblow**, where a lookout 100m from the car park looks over the sandblow towards the ocean. After wandering along the scribbly gum-lined track to the lookout, return to your vehicle and motor off towards the beach.

Southern Lakes Tourist Drive (Green)

29km, 2hr driving time

From Central Station, head south at the main crossroads. The track dives and soars past hoop pines and tall forests. Then it skirts moody **Lake Jennings**, and **Lake Birrabeen** with its famous twisted melaleuca on the foreshore.

The road continues past **Barga Lagoon** and the sometimes choppy **Lake Benaroon** before heading to **Lake Boomanjin**, with its famous patterned sands beneath the tannin waters. Turn left onto Dillingham's Road and head for Dilli Village and the ocean beach. Just before you get to Dilli, a deep creek crossing provides some unusual excitement.

Pile Valley

Sunset

Lake McKenzie

FRANK STOFFELS

Sunrise

Fishing

Fraser Island probably has the best beach fishing anywhere on the Australian coast. You only have to see the number of anglers standing hip-deep in surf along the eastern beach during the peak of the tailor season (August-September).

The estuary fishing along the west coast is sensational too (flathead, whiting, bream, and not to forget the juiciest mud crabs). The Roy Rufus Reef off Woody Island is another good spot – it's the largest artificial reef in the southern hemisphere, built to help stop the decline of the local fish population. The rocks and reefs off Indian Head and Middle Rocks, and further out on the continental shelf, are good for a wide variety of bottom and surface species (red emperor, coral trout, tuna and cod, to name just a few). The rocks off Waddy Point are very popular, and many fishers launch their boats from the beach in the lee of this outcrop. The calm waters behind Indian Head are another popular east-coast launching spot.

Beach fishing is done in the surf gutters between the beach and the sand banks, where the breaking surf stirs up food that attracts fish. For the best results, try low tide at dawn or dusk, and keep an eye out for birds such as crested terns over the most bountiful areas. Then again, you can also just make a beeline for where other fishers congregate...

The whiting fishing from July to March is the best in Queensland but the tailor season really draws the crowds. In the past this led to over-fishing which has now been curbed somewhat. The tailor catch limit is 20 in total for recreational fishers (or 30 during a stay on the island of 72 hours or more), with a minimum size of 30cm – tailor tastes best fresh so there's little point taking it home anyway. During the tailor spawning season from 1 August to 30 September (dates subject to change) all fishing is prohibited from 400m south of Indian Head to 400m north of Waddy Point, and 400m out from the low-water mark in this area.

Fish offal attracts dingoes and should be buried in the beach at least 50cm deep and well below the high-water mark. Simply depositing it in the sea attracts bronze whaler sharks that always seem to lurk scarily close to shore.

Those fishing on the eastern beach should be aware of stinging fireweed, especially with northerly winds – see p27. Fish avoid fireweed areas for good reason.

Note: No fishing or bait collecting is allowed in the island's lakes or streams.

Fishing off the rocks at Waddy Point

Further Information

- www.dpi.qld.gov.au/fishweb – the Queensland Department of Primary Industries' page for recreational fishing rules, with some useful links. You can also contact the DPI call centre on Ph 13 25 23. There's a toll-free Fishwatch Hotline to report suspected illegal fishing activities (not for general inquiries) on Ph 1800 017 116.
- www.fishnet.com.au – a useful sport fishing site. If you can't find what you're looking for in one of the many links and directories, it probably doesn't exist.
- www.fishingfraserisland.com – a good information resource for Fraser Island fishing
- www.fishingmonthly.com.au – useful information about Fraser Island in the Archives and Reports sections

Garrys Anchorage at low tide

Kingfisher Bay Resort

FRANK STOFFELS

Rentals & Charters

If you're already on the island, Kingfisher Bay Resort, Ph 1800 072 555, rents out to guests and non-guests motorised, dinghies that are ideal for fishing in the estuaries along the west coast.

On the mainland, **Rainbow Beach Fishing Charters**, Ph (07) 5486 8666, organises reef-fishing tours off the Cooloola and Fraser coasts. Quite a few sport and game-fishing charter boats also operate out of Hervey Bay.

Boating
Canoeing & Kayaking

Fraser Island's lakes are pleasant spots for a paddle, especially Lake McKenzie and some of the lakes up north (Ocean Lake springs to mind). Be careful not to damage the rushes and birds' nests, and wear protection against the fierce sun – but avoid sunscreen as it pollutes the pristine water.

The many inlets along the sheltered west coast are tailor-made for kayaking and canoeing, and sea kayakers can enjoy themselves in Hervey Bay and down the Great Sandy Strait.

Unfortunately, carrying a boat on top of a vehicle is difficult due to the bumpy roads and overhanging vegetation, which is why you don't see as many canoes or kayaks as you might expect.

Rentals & Tours

Kingfisher Bay Resort, Ph 1800 072 555, rents out canoes, also to non-guests. It also organises guided canoe paddles up Dundonga Creek to see the mangroves, and possibly dolphins, dugongs and sea birds along the way. These tours last an hour-and-a-half.

Aussie Sea Kayak Tours, Ph (07) 5452 7383, www.ausseakayak.com.au, runs three-day kayak tours out of Urangan or River Heads, taking in the Great Sandy Strait and the west coast of Fraser Island. The tours cater for beginners as well as experienced sea kayakers, and are a great adventure.

Yachting & Motor-Sailing

The sheltered west coast is literally a haven for yachties, as the number of boats moored at places such as Garrys Anchorage and Wathumba Creek will attest. (Both these spots, by the way, are ideal for meeting up with friends or relatives in a vehicle, so they can go on a cruise and you can explore the interior.)

Bear in mind that the tidal estuaries and Sandy Strait in general can be tricky, so you'll need some experience and good charts. Deep-keeled yachts won't be able to rest on the tidal flats easily – catamarans have the advantage here.

KINGFISHER BAY RESORT

Canoeing in Dundonga Creek

Rentals & Charters

Kingfisher Bay Resort rents out small catamarans, also to non-guests. For more serious yachts, motor cruisers and/or motorised houseboats, try the following, but note that prices are an indication only and don't include extras. Skippered charter tours are also available:

- **Fraser Escape Bareboat Charters**,
  Ph (07) 4125 7200
  www.fraserescape.com.au,
  admin@fraserescape.com.au
  Operates ex Hervey Bay

- **Rainbow Beach Houseboats**,
  Ph (07) 5486 3146
  www.rainbowbeachhouseboats.com.au,
  enquire@rainbowbeachhouseboats.com.au

- **Luxury Afloat**,
  Ph (07) 5486 4864,
  www.luxuryafloat.com.au,
  Tin Can Bay – luxurious houseboats

Swimming

The lakes and creeks are perfect for swimming, though snorkellers may be disappointed because there's little to see. A trip to Fraser would not be complete without a swim in one of the glorious lakes, such as Lake Birrabeen or Lake McKenzie, or a pleasant and relaxing ride with the fast-flowing current along Eli Creek.

Please keep in mind that sunscreens, insect repellents, soaps, detergents and skin creams pollute these pristine lakes. The water can get quite cold in the winter months, though the shallow window lakes (Ocean Lake, for example) are warmer.

Unfortunately you can't swim or surf off Fraser Island's magnificent eastern beach. It has deep gutters and some of the strongest rip currents in Australia, along with large numbers of sharks attracted to the bountiful fish and vigorous fishing activities. There are no lifeguards either. If you must swim on the east coast, try the Champagne Pools, but only around low tide and be careful on the slippery rocks. Beware of fireweed (see p27).

The calm, sheltered west coast is a bit safer (if perhaps less exciting) but has few accessible sections that aren't lined with mangroves and estuarine mud. Notable exceptions are some of the isolated camping areas between Moon Point and Wathumba, and the particularly beautiful section of beach north of Wathumba that can only be reached by walking along a 10km management track from Orchid Beach township.

Whale-Watching

This is one of the highlights of a visit to the island. Humpback whales regularly pass Indian Head during their autumn migration from the Antarctic to the Coral Sea, but Hervey Bay is the best place in the world to see them up close when they head down south again from August to October.

See Fauna in the earlier Backgrounds chapter for more about humpback whales and their migration patterns.

In late winter, many operators run whale-watching boat tours in the Hervey Bay Marine Park, which consists of Platypus Bay down to Moon Point and halfway out west to Bundaberg. The park was established in 1989 to manage human activities around whales. If you see the number of boats in the high season, it's easy to understand why this was necessary.

What To Do

Tours

Most tour boats operate from Hervey Bay. For an overview of the different mainland operators, click on the Whale-Watching link on www.frasercoastholidays.info.

On the island itself, the Kingfisher Bay resort, Ph 1800 372 737, runs daily tours in the whale season from 7.45am till noon. In the unlikely event that the whales don't show, you get another free trip. The resort also has a whale-watch cruise package that includes transfers from the mainland and two nights B&B at the resort.

Several companies run whale-watching flights from Hervey Bay Airport. While these are interesting and also give you a chance to see some of the island from up high, they don't provide the thrill of a close encounter with a whale, which can stay with you for life.

Sunshine Aviation, Ph (07) 5450 0516, offers both experiences on its day tours from Sunshine Coast (Mudgimba) Airport near Maroochydore. It flies you up to Hervey Bay for a catamaran tour and then takes you over the island before returning to Maroochydore.

Bird-Watching

Fraser Island is a prime bird-watching area, with one of the largest but also most varied bird communities in Australia. Almost half of the 750 bird species in Australia have been sighted here, and avid twitchers may observe well over 50 species in a day.

The best times are early morning after sunrise and mid to late afternoon. Many birds stick to specific habitats, so you'll increase your tally if you visit a variety of vegetation types.

Good bird-watching areas include, but are by no means limited to:

- Champagne Pools and Waddy Point area – wrens and small woodland and coastal birds, roosting spots near Waddy Point
- Wetlands near Kingfisher Bay and anywhere along the west coast – migratory waders from Siberia, ibis, spoonbills
- Wathumba Creek – rare beach curlew
- Basin Lake
- Eastern beach – white-breasted sea eagles, brahminy kites, pied oystercatchers, dotterels, crested terns, ospreys
- Inland forests – lorikeets, cockatoos, tawny frogmouths, owls

The Kingfisher Bay Resort organises bird-watching walks (including a Birding for Beginners Walk), as well as a Bird Week each May, with excursions, talks by visiting specialists, and photography and art sessions related to birds. For information, Ph 1800 072 555, http://birdwatching.kingfisherbay.com.

A close encounter with a whale is an experience that stays with you for life

KINGFISHER BAY RESORT

Organised Tours

Commercial sightseeing tours are available from Rainbow Beach, the Sunshine Coast, Hervey Bay and Brisbane, and on the island from the Kingfisher Bay and Eurong resorts. Most of these take one or two days and provide an affordable, quick overview of the highlights. Many operators use 4WD buses that carry 10 to 50 passengers.

Several companies offer walking, safari or specialised tours, some of which can last up to a week. Kingfisher Bay Resort also offers private tours where one of its rangers accompanies you in your vehicle. Scenic helicopter and plane flights over the island depart from Hervey Bay and the beach at Eurong, Happy Valley, Eli Creek and Cathedral Beach.

For further details, refer to the activities earlier in this chapter or in the Getting Around chapter, inquire through travel agents (see Tourist Offices and Useful Websites pp37-38), or contact the following operators direct:

- **Air Fraser Island**
  Ph (07) 4125 3600,
  www.airfraserisland.com.au, airfraser@bigpond.com
- **Australian Day Tours**
  Ph (07) 3489 6400,
  www.daytours.com.au,
  reservations@daytours.com.au
- **Blue Dolphin Marine Tours**
  Ph (07) 4124 9600,
  www.bluedolphintours.com.au
- **Fraser Exclusive Tours**
  Ph 1800 063 933, (07) 4125 3933,
  www.fraserislandco.com.au

- **Fraser Explorer Tours**
  Ph 1800 372 737,
  www.fraserexplorertours.com.au
- **Fraser Island Adventure Tours/Fraser Island Getaway 4x4 Tours**
  Ph (07) 5444 6957,
  www.tourfraser.com.au,
  info@tourfraser.com.au
- **Fraser Island Discovery**
  Ph (07) 5449 0393,
  www.fraserislanddiscovery.com.au,
  info@fraserislanddiscovery.com.au
- **Fraser Island Trailblazer Tours**
  Ph 1800 639 518, (07) 5499 9505,
  www.trailblazertours.com.au,
  info@trailblazertours.com.au
- **Goanna Adventures**
  Ph (07) 3841 7781,
  www.goannaadventures.com.au,
  bookings@goannaadventures.com.au
- **Kingfisher Bay Resort**
  Ph 1800 372 737,
  www.kingfisherbay.com,
  reservations@kingfisherbay.com
- **MI Helicopters**
  Ph (07) 4125 1599
  www.mihelicopters.com.au
- **Sunshine Aviation**
  Ph (07) 5450 0516,
  www.sunshineaviation.com,
  tours@sunshineaviation.com.au
- **Sunrover Expeditions**
  Ph 1800 353 717,
  www.sunrover.com.au,
  tours@sunrover.com.au

FRANK STOFFELS

Photography

Fraser Island yells out to be photographed and you're likely to gobble up film. Print film is readily available (check the use-by date) but slide film less so – bring plenty of the latter and/or digital memory for the video and digital camera. Memory devices can be expensive, but a laptop will let you store digital photos as you go.

When taking photographs, allow for the intensity of the light which washes out the colours. All that water and white sand makes matters worse. You can compensate for this to some extent with a polarising filter (tricky!), but it's always best to photograph in the early morning or late afternoon. Low light brings out the colours and dramatic shadows, which makes for better shots anyway. Refer to your camera manual for exposure settings against bright backgrounds, in order to avoid little Jenny's adorable face turning out too dark on the Lake McKenzie beach.

Keep film cool, especially after exposure. Clothes provide good insulation, so a bag of film rolls stuffed among the clothes in your luggage should suffice. Some people store film in the esky or portable fridge, which is fine so long as it is kept in a separate, waterproof container (not just the standard film canisters), and is allowed to come up to temperature to prevent condensation problems before going into the camera.

Beware of sand getting into the camera – a simple cleaning kit with a puff brush is a wise investment – and wipe off any salt spray immediately. It's always a good idea to protect the lens with a UV or skylight filter.

If you have a digital camera and take photos of moving objects (a breaching whale, for instance), bear in mind that the mechanism takes a while to prime itself, so you'll miss the action unless you preset focus and exposure or prime the frame in advance. Refer to your camera manual.

Fun for Kids

There are few outdoor destinations in Australia better suited to a family holiday than Fraser Island. It never takes long to get from A to B, and there are plenty of areas where you can go for a swim (kids love Eli Creek) or paddle, or a short walk or exploration. Toddlers can play just about anywhere in the world's biggest sandbox.

Playgrounds can be found at Kingfisher Bay, Eurong and Cathedral Beach. Kingfisher Bay Resort goes out of its way to keep children occupied, with Junior Eco Ranger programmes (weekends and school holidays) that are free to guests' children aged 5 to 14 years, learn-to-fish courses, tennis courts, canoes, and even a purpose-built Kids' Club for babies to five-year-olds (all year, 8am to 4pm).

Out in the bush, however, stay with your children at all times, especially at potentially dangerous spots such as Indian Head (high cliff) and anywhere they could go wandering off, and keep them well away from dingoes. Campers with children under 14 should stay at fenced camping areas (Central Station, Dilli Village, Lake Boomanjin and Waddy Point). ■

Playing at Eli Creek

ROB BOEGHEIM

What To Do

Index

Text References

- **bold** page numbers –
  major references
- normal page numbers –
  references (minor references
  ignored)

A

Aborigines,
  see Butchulla people
acacias 19, **23**
access 55
accommodation **47–53**
acid frogs, *see* frogs
activities **85–108**
aircraft, *see* flying
angiopteris ferns 20, *20*
animals, *see* fauna
apartments,
  see holiday houses, resorts
Aquarium, the, *see*
  Champagne Pools
ATMs, *see* EFTPOS

B

Badtjala, *see* Butchulla people
Balarrgan (North White Cliffs)
  8, 9, 12, **83**
bangalow palms,
  see piccabeen palms
banksias 19, 20, **23–24**
Barga Lagoon 90, 100
barges **56–57**
Barnewall, Sir Reginald 13
barrage lakes **18**
bars, *see* resorts
Basin Lake **70**, 88, 95, 106
bats **28–29**
B&B, *see* holiday houses, resorts
beaches, *see* geography
beach spinifex 19, **25**
bicycle **65**
Big Woody Island 9
Binngih Sandblow **77**
birds 32, **30–32**, 58,
  106–107
bird-watching **106–107**,
  see also birds
boating 55, **104–105**
Bogimbah (Creek) 9, 11,13, 16,
  20, 97
books 39
Bool Creek 9

Boomerang Lakes *6, 16*, 17, 98
Boon Boon Creek 76
boronias **26**
Bowarrady Trail **86**
Breaksea Spit 9, 35, **79**
brumbies **30**
Buff Creek 13, 83
bushfire 22, 85
bushwalking **65**, **85–97**
Butchulla people **8**, 9, 30, 39,
  42, **48**, 70, **76**

C

cabins, *see* holiday houses,
  resorts
campfires, *see* firewood
camping 40, 41, *41*, **47–49**, 55,
  108
camping gas (propane) 47, 59
camping permits **41**
cane toads 32, 33
canoeing **104**
cars, *see* driving
casuarinas, *see* horsetail
  she-oaks
Cathedral Beach (coastline) **75**
Cathedral Beach (Resort &
  Camping Park) 9, 44, 45, **48**,
  51, 108
Cathedrals, the 7, **75**
Central Lakes Tourist Drive 68,
  70, **101**
Central Station 7, 12, 25, 37,
  67–68, 88, 90, 95, 96, 101
Champagne Pools (the
  Aquarium) *6*, 53, **77**, 105,
  106
children **108**
climate **39–40**
coastal banksias, *see* banksias
coffee rock **15**, 79
communication **44**
Cook, Captain James **9**, 76
Cooloola 10, 13, 23, 55
Cooloola monster **33**
Coolooloi Creek 49
Coomboo Lake,
  see Lake Coomboo
Coongul Creek 80
cottages,
  see holiday houses, resorts
courtesy **64**
crowds **40**
cycling **65**
cypress pines 19

D

dangers, *see* precautions
Declivity, the 98
Deep Creek 49, **83**
diesel 59
Dillingham's Road 7, 13, 100
Dilli Village 7, 13, 47, 93, 95,
  100
dingoes 27–28, **29**, 47, 108
dining **45**,
  see also resorts
driving 55, **57–64**, **97–101**
dolphins **35**
dugongs **36**
Dundonga Creek 8, 104
Dundubara 7, 47, 75, 86
dunes, *see* sand (formations)

E

eastern beach, *see*
  Seventy-Five Mile Beach
ecosystems, *see* geography
Edwardson, Captain William 9
EFTPOS 45
Eli Creek *6, 54*, 65, **73**, 105
emergencies **44**
environmental concerns
  42, 47, 57, **58**
EPA offices **37**
eucalypts 19, 23
Eurong (Beach Resort) 7, 13,
  37, 44–45, 50, **52**, 65, 72, 107,
  108

F

fauna **27–30**
fens **22**
ferries **55–57**
FIDO 13, **37**, 38
Fig Tree Point 49
film, *see* photography
fire, *see* bushfire, firewood
fireweed **27**
firewood 42
first aid **44**
fish 17, 18, **36**,
  see also fishing
fishing 7, 52, 53, 77, **103–104**,
  see also fish
Flinders, Matthew 9
Flinders Sandblow **79**
flora **23–29**
flying **65**
food **45**
foredunes **18–19**, **25–26**
  see also geography

Index

map references

Places/features listed here are those mentioned in the text and included in the map extents – others are not referenced.

They are indicated by page number followed by their grid reference – e.g. "122, D3" means page 122, grid D3.

Index

Fraser Island Maps

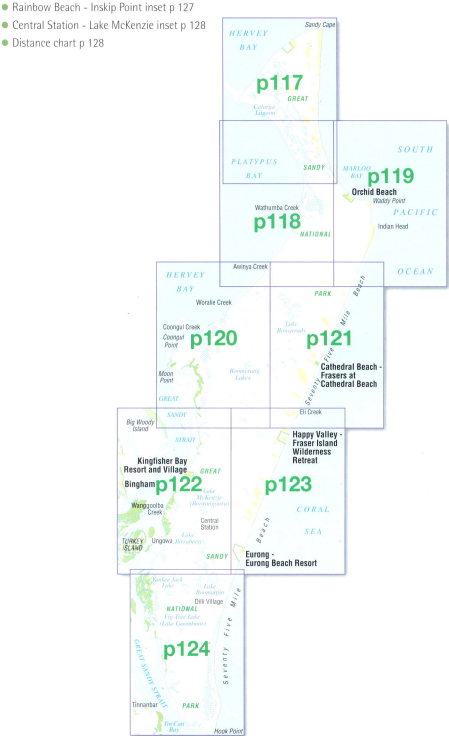

Waddy Point
ROB BOEGHEIM

legend

ROADS AND TRACKS

Major Road	*sealed* *unsealed*
Minor Road	*sealed* *unsealed*
Major Track	
Minor Track	
Overgrown Track	
Track - Management use only/Gate	
Walking Track	
Fraser Island Great Walk/Feeder Track	
Built Up Area	
Beach Camping Zone	
Aircraft Landing Zone	
No Vehicle Zone	
40kmph Shared Zone	
Total Kilometres	★ 18 ★
Intermediate Kilometres	6
National/State Route Numbers	1 85

OTHER FEATURES

Tourist Point of Interest/Building

National Park Boundary

Marine Park Boundary

Lake - Perennial/Intermittent

Swamp

Contours (with value in metres) — 40

Sand

Mangroves/State Forest

SERVICES

Information Centre/Ranger Station

Emergency First Aid/Telephone

Bush Fire Brigade/Postal

SUPPLIES

General Store/Bottled Gas

Unleaded and Diesel Fuel Available

Meals/Bar or Liquor Supplies/Ice

FACILITIES

Accommodation Resort/Private

Backpacker Accommodation

Camping Area - EPA - Designated/Bush

             - Privately Managed

No Camping Permitted

Camper Trailer Site

Toilet Waste Disposal Facility

Caravan Park

Police Station

Showers

Toilets

Picnic Area

Gas Barbecue/Communal fire ring

Mechanical Repairs

Compressed Air

Boat Launching Site

Rubbish Disposal or Bin Provided

Water (treat before drinking)

EFTPOS

TRANSPORTATION

Barge Landing

Boat Anchorage

Passenger Ferry or Water Taxi

Airport/Airfield or Beach Landing

Helipad

ACTIVITIES

Lookout or Viewpoint

Walking Track

No swimming

Fishing (popular spot)

Canoeing

Lighthouse

Shipwreck (may be submerged)

SCALE 1:130,000

0 km   1   2   3   4   5   10   15 km

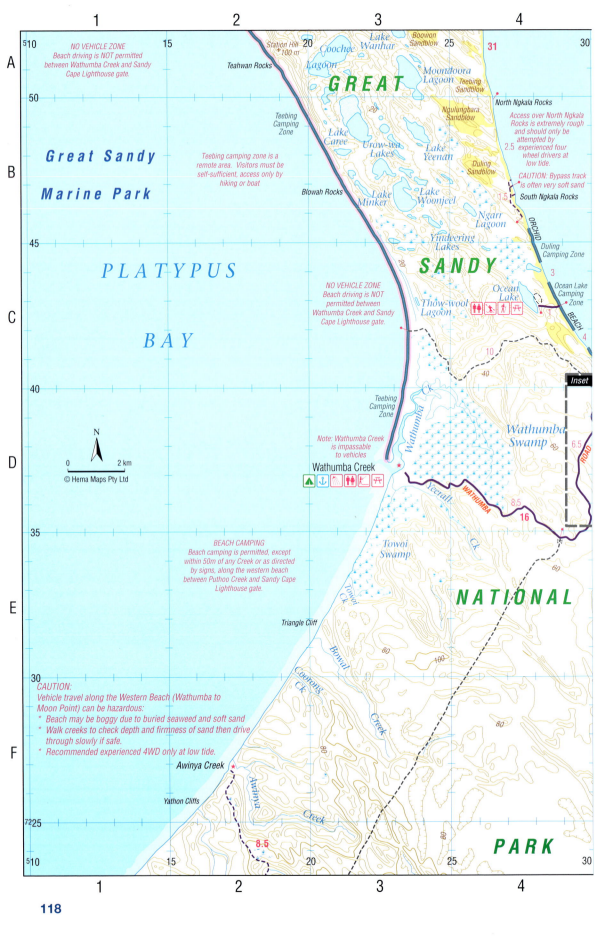

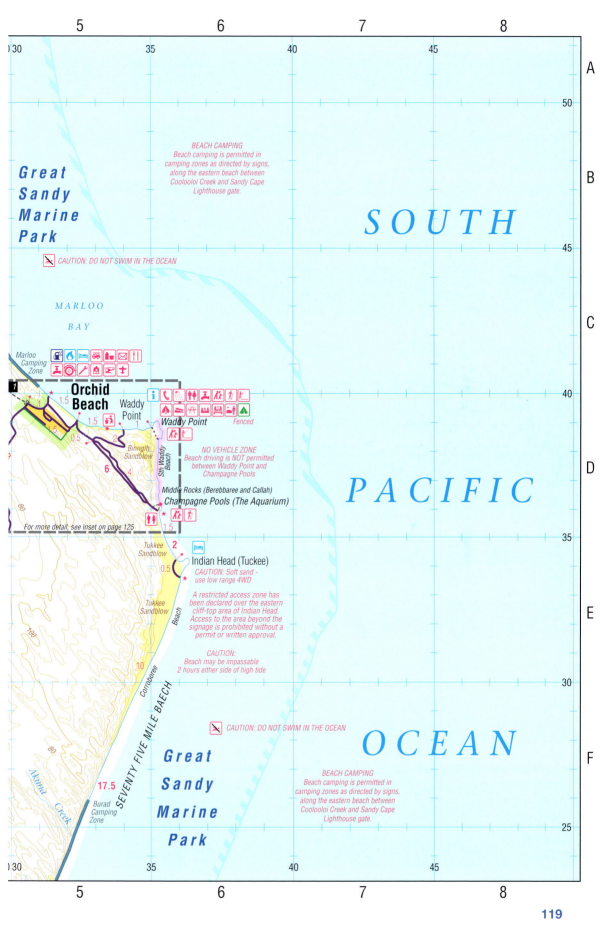

Great Sandy Marine Park

BEACH CAMPING
Beach camping is permitted in camping zones as directed by signs, along the eastern beach between Cooloooloi Creek and Sandy Cape Lighthouse gate.

SOUTH

PACIFIC

OCEAN

CAUTION: DO NOT SWIM IN THE OCEAN

MARLOO BAY

Marloo Camping Zone

Orchid Beach

Waddy Point

Waddy Point   Fenced

1.5
1.5
0.5
2
6
4

Binngih Sandblow

Sth Waddy Beach

NO VEHICLE ZONE
Beach driving is NOT permitted between Waddy Point and Champagne Pools

Middle Rocks (Berebbaree and Callah)
Champagne Pools (The Aquarium)

For more detail, see inset on page 125

1.5

Tukkee Sandblow

2

Indian Head (Tuckee)

0.5

CAUTION: Soft sand - use low range 4WD

A restricted access zone has been declared over the eastern cliff-top area of Indian Head. Access to the area beyond the signage is prohibited without a permit or written approval.

CAUTION:
Beach may be impassable 2 hours either side of high tide

Tukkee Sandblow

Beach

Corroboree

SEVENTY FIVE MILE BEACH

80

100

10

CAUTION: DO NOT SWIM IN THE OCEAN

Great Sandy Marine Park

17.5

Burad Camping Zone

Akuna Creek

BEACH CAMPING
Beach camping is permitted in camping zones as directed by signs, along the eastern beach between Cooloooloi Creek and Sandy Cape Lighthouse gate.

80

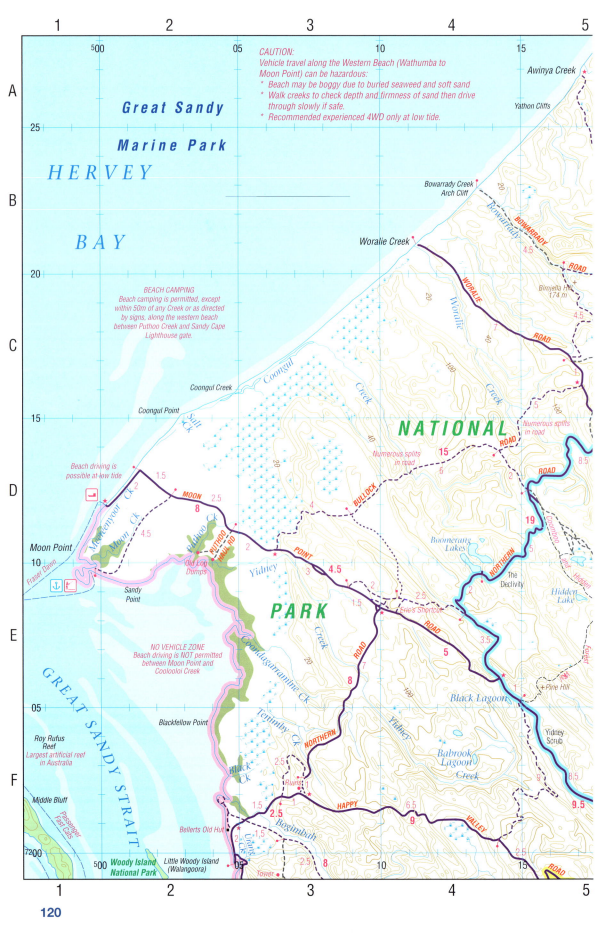

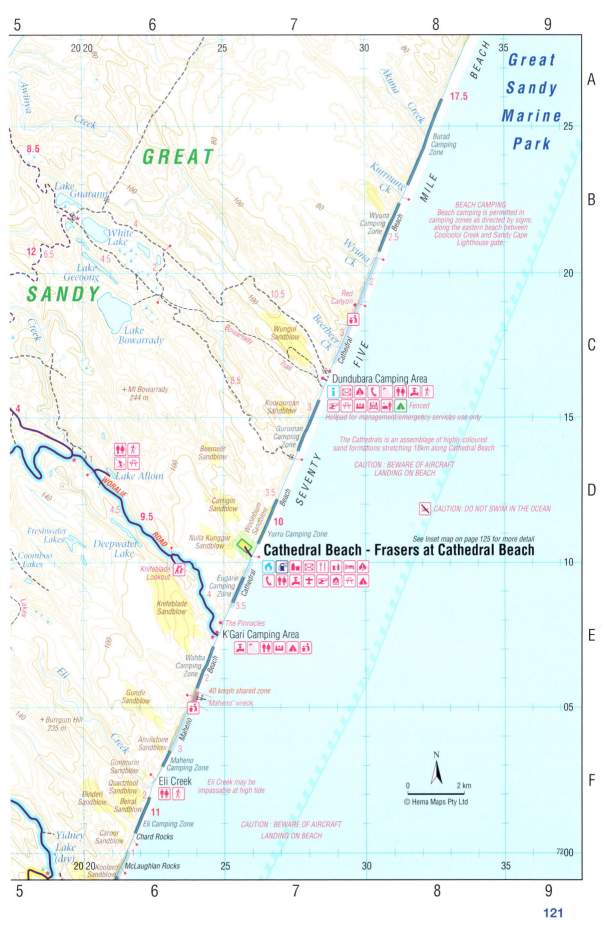

Great Sandy Strait / Fraser Island map

Grid columns: 1, 2, 3, 4

Grid rows: A, B, C, D, E, F

Woody Island National Park 95 20 500 05 10
Urangan Boat Harbour
Passenger Fast Cats
Big Woody Island
Middle Bluff
GREAT
Ruins
HAPPY
Bogimbah
2.5
8
BOGIMBAH
Tower
Disused Bogimbah Airstrip
4.5
SANDY
10
Bellerts Old Hut
Little Woody Island (Walangoora)
Woody Island National Park
Bogimbah
SANDY
NORTHERN
POSTANS
(POYUNGAN)
5
Poyungan Hill 180 m
7200
Great Sandy Marine Park
South Point
STRAIT
Log Landing
Poyungan
Creek
Poyungan Forestry Camp (Ruins)
0.5
60
Boon
Picnic Island
Duck Island
ROAD
6
Boon
100
Mangrove Point
95
Booral
NO VEHICLE ZONE
Beach driving is NOT permitted between Moon Point and Coolooloi Creek
Dundonga
NATIONAL
Creek
1.5
Leading Hill 184 m
SMITH
Mangrove Islands
CORNWELLS
6
8.5
RD
Kingfisher Bay Resort and Village
See Inset on page 126 for more detail
North White Cliffs
Former Z Force Commandos training site
McKenzies Jetty and Mill (ruins)
Balarrgan
Mission Site
Dundonga
ROAD
NORTHERN
Sleeber Hill
90
Bingham
River Heads
Barge
Kingfisher
Fraser
PARK
BENNETT
5.5
Lake McKenzie (Boorangoora)
NORTHERN
120
North Head
South Head
Shoulder Point
Venture
Duck CK
Fire Control Line
Inset 7
LAKE
5
McKENZIE RD
5
For more detail, see map on page 128
85
Mary River
Wanggoolba Creek
WANGGOOLBA
2.5
ROAD
Wanggoolba
Hiker's Camp
Hiker's Camp
Central Station Campground
Central Station
Pile Valley
80 Lakes Forest 100
NO VEHICLE ZONE
Beach driving is NOT permitted between Coolooloi Creek and Moon Point
Panama Ck
Rocky
Little Rocky Ck
2.5
ROAD
(Woongoorra)
Basin Lake
8
3
BIRRABEEN
4.5
8.5
Maaroom Fish Habitat Reserve
Walsh Island
UNGOWA
6
7.5
OLD
ROCKY CREEK
RD
80
140
4
Lake Jennings
Lake Birrabeen
10.5
TURKEY ISLAND
Ungowa
Jetty (condemned)
South White Cliffs
Deep Creek
Buff Creek
Bookar Island
Ungowa Ck
Allisator Creek
Ceratodus Ck
2
Hiker's Camp
Lake Barga
Lake Benaroon
3.5
ROAD
Maaroom Fish Habitat Reserve
SOUTHERN ROAD
Buff Ck
Cibbin Ck
4.5
80
Yankee
Deep Ck
DILLINGHAMS
Jack or Tunbowah Creek
Mr Boomanjin 211 m
Road
100
100
4.5
22
Lake Boomanjin
7175
95
500
10
05
10

122

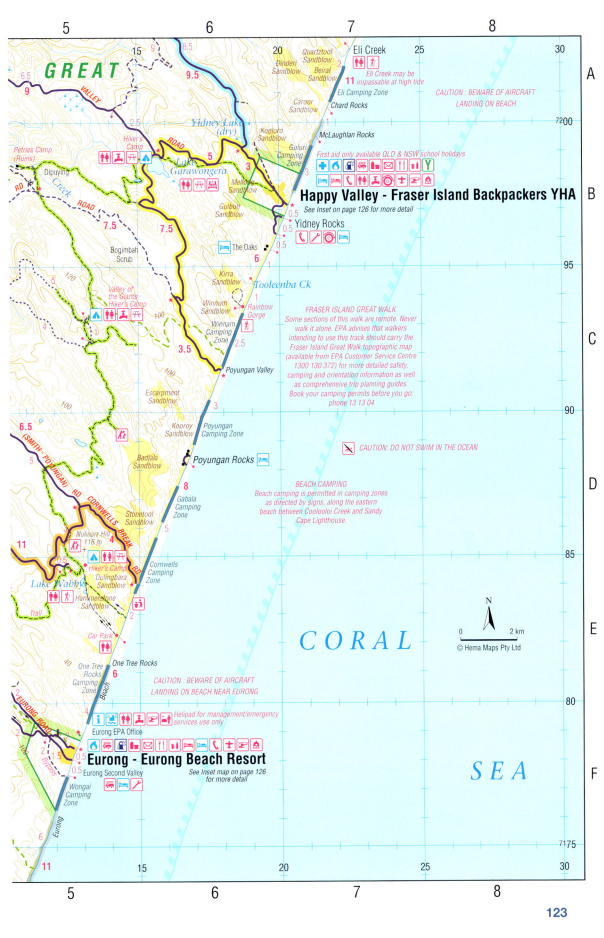

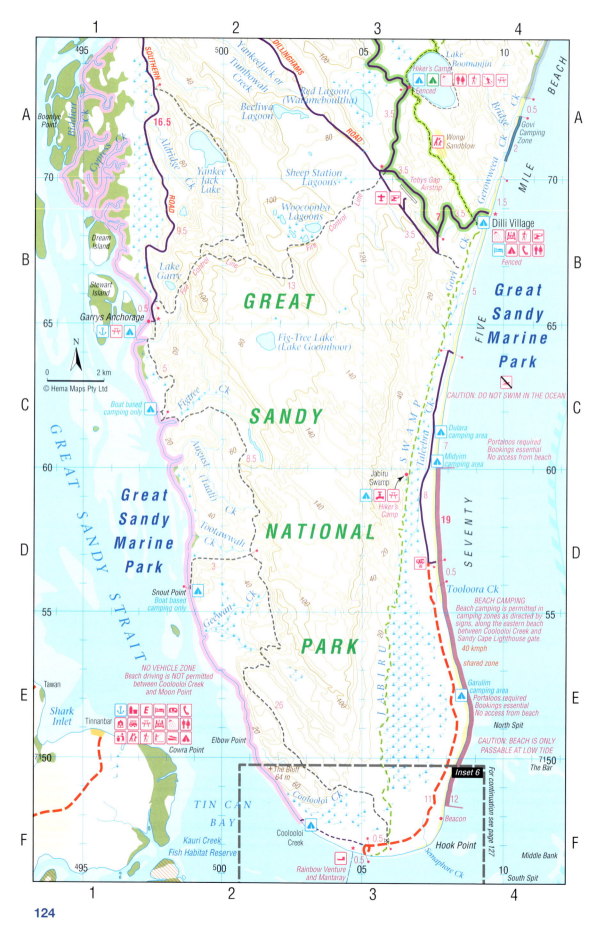

1   **2**   **3**   **4**

A

Boonlye Point

Biddiri Ck

Cypress Ck

495

SOUTHERN

500

Yankeeluck or Tumbowah Creek

DILLINGHAMS

100

05

10

BEACH

Lake Boomanjin

Hiker's Camp

Fenced

Wongi Sandblow

16.5

Alabridge Ck

40

80

Beeliwa Lagoon

Red Lagoon (Wabimeboultha)

3.5

Bridge Ck

0.5

Govi Camping Zone

2

MILE

A

70

Dream Island

Yankee Jack Lake

9.5

80

100

Sheep Station Lagoons

Woocoonba Lagoons

Fire Control Line

Line

Tobys Gap Airstrip

3.5

7

3.5

3.5

Geonwea Ck

1.5

Dilli Village

Fenced

70

B

Stewart Island

Lake Garry

0.5

Garrys Anchorage

13

Fire Control Line

400

120

20

5

Govi Ck

Great Sandy Marine Park

65

B

65

GREAT

80

Fig-Tree Lake (Lake Goomboor)

140

FIVE

CAUTION: DO NOT SWIM IN THE OCEAN

C

Boat based camping only

5

60

Figtree Ck

SANDY

20

140

8.5

SWAMP

40

Talebra Ck

Dulara camping area

7

Midyim camping area

Portaloos required
Bookings essential
No access from beach

60

C

N

0   2 km

© Hema Maps Pty Ltd

60

D

Snout Point

Boat based camping only

Great Sandy Marine Park

August (Tuali) Ck

40

Tootawwah Ck

3

NATIONAL

60

140

20

40

8

19

SEVENTY

Jabiru Swamp

Hiker's Camp

0.5

Tooloora Ck

D

55

GREAT SANDY STRAIT

Geewan Ck

40

PARK

26

20

20

LABIRU

BEACH CAMPING
Beach camping is permitted in
camping zones as directed by
signs, along the eastern beach
between Coolooloi Creek and
Sandy Cape Lighthouse gate.

40 kmph

shared zone

55

E

Tawan

Shark Inlet

Tinnanbar

Cowra Point

NO VEHICLE ZONE
Beach driving is NOT permitted
between Coolooloi Creek
and Moon Point

Elbow Point

20

100

Garulim camping area
Portaloos required
Bookings essential
No access from beach

North Spit

CAUTION: BEACH IS ONLY
PASSABLE AT LOW TIDE

E

7150

495

The Bluff
64 m

60

Coolooloi Ck

Inset 6

The Bar

7150

For continuation see page 127

F

TIN CAN BAY

Kauri Creek
Fish Habitat Reserve

Coolooloi Creek

Rainbow Venture
and Mantaray

0.5

500

0.5

05

11

12

Beacon

Samaphore Ck

Hook Point

Middle Bank

South Spit

F

1   **2**   **3**   **4**

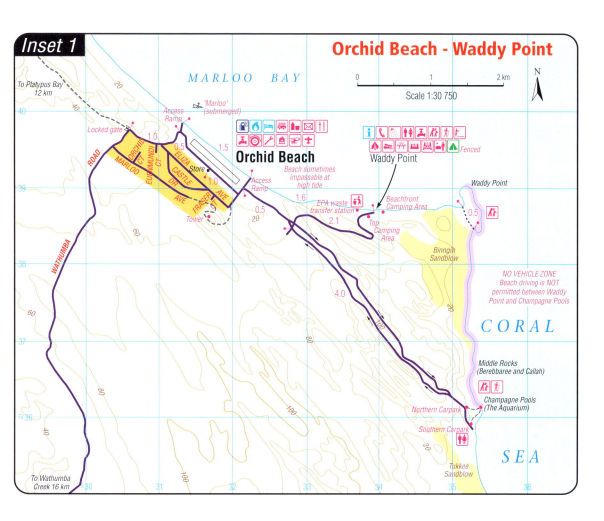

Orchid Beach - Waddy Point

Inset 1

MARLOO BAY

Scale 1:30 750

0   1   2 km

N

To Platypus Bay
12 km

"Marloo"
(submerged)

Access
Ramp

Locked gate

ROAD

ORCHID CT

EUMUNDI CT

ELIZA CT

CASTLE DR

MARLOO AVE

FRASER CT

AVE

Store

Orchid Beach

Waddy Point

Fenced

Waddy Point

Access
Ramp

Tower

20

Beach sometimes
impassable at
high tide

EPA waste
transfer station

Beachfront
Camping Area

Top
Camping
Area

Binngih
Sandblow

WATHUMBA

60

60

80

100

NO VEHICLE ZONE
Beach driving is NOT
permitted between Waddy
Point and Champagne Pools

C O R A L

Middle Rocks
(Berebbaree and Callah)

Northern Carpark

Southern Carpark

Champagne Pools
(The Aquarium)

S E A

Tukkee
Sandblow

To Wathumba
Creek 16 km

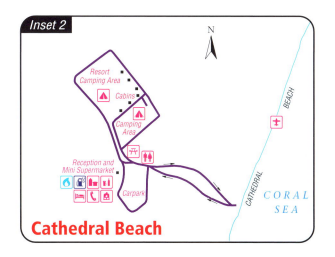

Inset 2

N

Resort
Camping Area

Cabins

Camping
Area

Reception and
Mini Supermarket

Carpark

BEACH

CATHEDRAL

C O R A L
S E A

Cathedral Beach

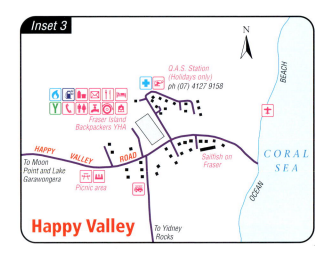

Happy Valley

Inset 3

Q.A.S. Station
(Holidays only)
ph (07) 4127 9158

Fraser Island
Backpackers YHA

HAPPY VALLEY ROAD

To Moon
Point and Lake
Garawongera

Picnic area

Sailfish on
Fraser

CORAL
SEA

OCEAN

BEACH

To Yidney
Rocks

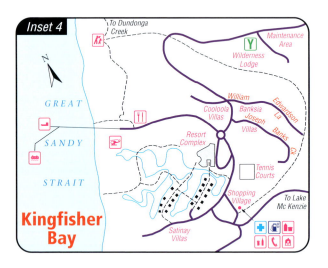

Kingfisher Bay

Inset 4

To Dundonga
Creek

Maintenance
Area

Wilderness
Lodge

William

Cooloola
Villas

Banksia

Joseph
Villas

Edwardson La

Banks Ck

GREAT

SANDY

STRAIT

Resort
Complex

Tennis
Courts

Shopping
Village

To Lake
Mc Kenzie

Satinay
Villas

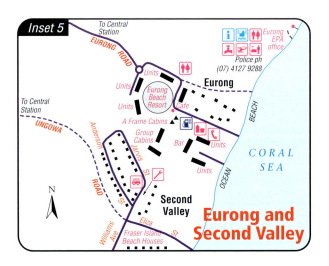

Eurong and Second Valley

Inset 5

To Central
Station

EURONG ROAD

Eurong
EPA
office

Police ph
(07) 4127 9288

Units

Units

Units

Eurong
Beach
Resort

Units

Eurong

Cafe

To Central
Station

UNGOWA

A Frame Cabins

Group
Cabins

Bar

Anderson

Jarvis St

Units

Units

ROAD

Williams Ave

Eliza St

**Second
Valley**

Fraser Island
Beach Houses

CORAL
SEA

OCEAN

BEACH

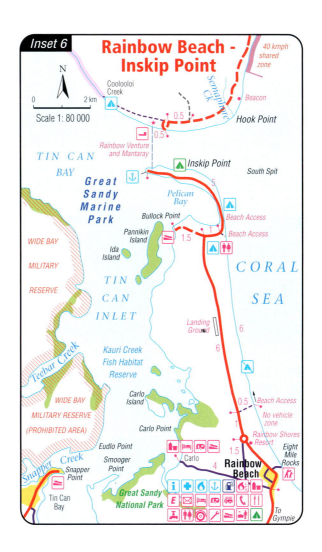

Inset 6

Rainbow Beach - Inskip Point

40 kmph shared zone

N

0 — 2 km

Scale 1: 80 000

Cooloooloi Creek

Semaphore Ck

Beacon

0.5

Hook Point

0.5

Rainbow Venture and Mantaray

Inskip Point

South Spit

T I N   C A N

B A Y

Great Sandy Marine Park

Pelican Bay

Beach Access

Bullock Point

Beach Access

Pannikin Island

1.5

WIDE BAY

Ida Island

MILITARY

T I N

RESERVE

C A N

I N L E T

C O R A L

S E A

Kauri Creek Fish Habitat Reserve

Landing Ground

6

6

Carlo Island

WIDE BAY

MILITARY RESERVE

(PROHIBITED AREA)

Carlo Point

Beach Access

0.5

No vehicle zone

Eudlo Point

Carlo

1

Rainbow Shores Resort

Smooger Point

Rainbow Beach

1.5

Eight Mile Rocks

Snapper Creek

Snapper Point

4

Tin Can Bay

Great Sandy National Park

E

To Gympie

127

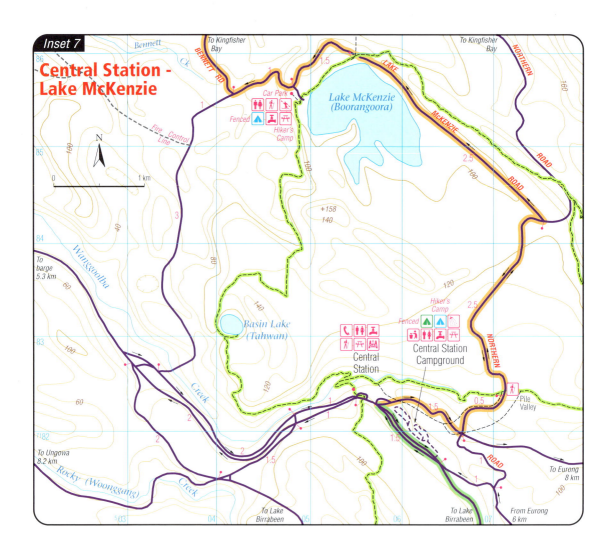

Inset 7

Central Station - Lake McKenzie

Distance Chart

Note: Distances may vary depending on tyre pressure and wheel-slip in soft sand.

133.5	108.5	97.5	106	111	77.5	63	39	31	Sandy Cape
102.5	77.5	66.5	75	80	46.5	32	8		Orchid Beach
94.5	69.5	58.5	67	72	38.5	24			Indian Head
70.5	45.5	34.5	43	48	14.5				Cathedral Beach
56	31	20	28.5	33.5					Happy Valley
58.5	33.5	22.5	14						Kingfisher Bay
44.5	19.5	8.5							Central Station
36	11								Eurong
25									Dilli Village

Hook Point